SLAVE TO THE VINE

Confessions of a Vagabond Cellarhand

"'Cause there's still a lot of wine and lonely girls
In this best of all possible worlds."

—*Kris Kristofferson*

AUTHOR'S NOTE

Slave to the Vine: Confessions of a Vagabond Cellarhand is a work of non-fiction and therefore a product of my own self-medicated memory. Out of respect, most names and identifying details have been changed.

SLAVE TO THE VINE

Confessions of a Vagabond Cellarhand

DARREN DELMORE

HELLMORE PRESS

San Luis Obispo, CA 93401
© 2016 by Darren Delmore

Library of Congress Cataloging-in-Publication Data is available.

ISBN-13: 978-0692550632

Book Design by Kenny Boyer

www.darrendelmore.com

Printed in the United States
Digit on the right indicates the number of this printing.
10 9 8 7 6 5 4 3 2

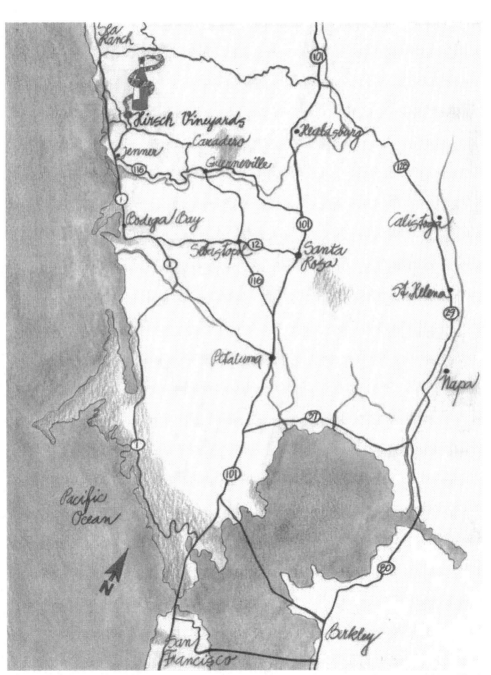

Illustration by Marie Hirsch

"Life is an uncertain proposition."

—*David Hirsch*

CHAPTER 1

I stumbled upon the crowded Hirsch Vineyards table at a springtime wine tasting event in Shell Beach, California. At that point of my existence, a premature midlife crisis was unfolding before me. I was about to turn 31 years old, was already wounded in the form of divorce and bad credit, and the theme park of a tasting room that I managed in Central California was turning me off of the wine industry and worsening my stomach condition by the pour. In short, I wasn't spitting as much wine out as I should have in a hot tent featuring 80-plus wineries pouring nothing but pricey Pinot Noir.

There was a hat-wearing, salt and pepper mustached man in a button-up shirt with an unmistakable smirk that I recognized from wine magazines. It was David Hirsch, the true Sonoma Coast grape-growing pioneer whose remote vineyard of Pinot Noir and Chardonnay was likened to American *Grand Cru* status by wine collectors and world famous wine critic Robert Parker alike. David and a woman in a sleeveless charcoal dress with cropped, jet-black hair and striking blue eyes were behind the small table, their empty bottles on display and wine-stained mailing list sign-up cards scattered about. Over a Hawaiian shirt-covered shoulder, I asked for a pour of their Estate Pinot Noir out of the decanter, then acted upon the urge to introduce myself as a guy whose first wine job was with a tiny winery that bought grapes from him years ago.

"I used to work for Tasha at Whitethorn," I said amid the accumulative roar. Most people around us were clearly plowed and boasting cheese-speckled faces, so as he listened to me, he looked as if he expected me to say something sinister. But as he put it together, and the place of Whitethorn Winery registered in his brain, I continued with the introduction. "I'm Darren."

He used his last name in his reply. "I'm David Hirsch." We shook hands, and he turned to the woman beside him and said, "Hey Marie, this guy used to work for Tasha."

"Oh really?" she asked in an excited accent, laughing wildly for some reason. Maybe they'd been working on their house palates, and with a swirl and whiff of their Pinot, I couldn't blame them. Aromatically alone, this wine stood out in a sea of amazing wines.

"Yeah, and actually, I'd left a message for you a few years back to see if you needed a harvest intern that year," I said to David. "I remember seeing an ad for it online. I ended up working at Bonny Doon Vineyard in Santa Cruz that year."

"Santa Cruz? Far out. I used to live there," David said, his eyes drifting up and away as he tripped out on the Whitethorn connection. "So you worked for Tasha? Ha! That's alright."

Maybe it was the fact that I'd already tasted over 60 wines, or that my job was getting to me in more ways than one. Or it could've well been the hash my friend and I had inhaled on the way to the tasting with death metal blaring, but I subconsciously delivered the fateful question: "So are you looking for somebody this year?"

"This year?" David paused to think about it. "Can you drive a forklift?" He smiled with all of his face on that one, and his eyes darted off left and right. Volunteers for the event were now coming by and chewing out wineries that were still pouring wine after the five o'clock cutoff. One woman shouted at David for doing it, and he rolled his eyes at her and poured a couple women next to me some wine anyhow.

"Forklift certified," I proudly announced, thinking how funny that sounded coming from me. Then, in my inebriation, I thought of how there are probably some dive bars in America where a man can get laid for boasting about such a qualification.

He handed me his card and said, "Give me a call, and I'll have you come out and see the site. It's great. You'd get to live out there." I took it gladly and, as more lushes crowded up for a last pour, thanked him again and told him I'd be in touch.

"You're in there bro," my wine slinger friend Trevor said to me as we walked away. The event was clearing out. We saw Gray Hartley from Hitching Post Winery packing up and Trevor went up to say bye to him. Gray handed over a half full bottle of Cargasacchi Vineyard Pinot Noir, and Trevor and I walked along the cliff with our thrashed Riedel goblets full of it, taking in the warm, central coast afternoon and the field of opportunity.

CHAPTER 2

I dove into the world of wine when I couldn't afford any of it. After a short stint in surf publishing and beer writing, I found myself newly wed and residing in crystal-meth colored Eureka, California. Though the nearest tasting room was 200 miles away, I spent my free time in Humboldt County absorbing every wine book and magazine that I could get my hands on. I got published in *Wine Spectator Magazine* and was astounded by my memory of each wine I consumed. There was clearly something passionate happening here. I made the decision to either get a job at a wine shop or learn how to make it.

I began working part time at Whitethorn Winery in June of 2001. As many occurrences in the emerald triangle of Northern California seem to play out, it was a metaphysical coincidence. I was unemployed in Eureka's infamously dismal job market and happened to be home one morning in mid-May listening to KMUD FM radio, smoking weed and drinking dark roast coffee, when an interview show came on featuring the three McKee sisters from the town of Whitethorn, California. In addition to describing their upbringing on a commune in South Humboldt County, Tasha McKee talked about her winery and how she relied on the local community for help during the harvest months. I'd seen the Whitethorn wines on the local retail shelves fetching the steepest price tags of the random Humboldt County wine producers. Interestingly enough, she was sourcing grapes for her wines from Carneros and the Sonoma Coast and trucking them four hours north to ferment on her family's isolated property.

On air Tasha mentioned how she'd love to have someone who was passionate about wine and willing to work join the process. Apparently, the locals were busy enough with their own sort of seasonal, "medicinal" harvest work, so any consistent assistant would be a blessing for her. I didn't see the winery number in the phone book, so I called the radio station and asked if they had a phone number. They didn't provide it, but took a message and gave it to her in person. I got a call from her a month later in the evening, and soon got the impression that I was talking to a very stoned woman. Her lengthy pauses and unclear directions about the amount of work she could offer me seemed very up in the air. Then she apologized and laughed, saying that she was battling a scorpion on her doorstep. She invited me down to see the winery and barrel taste some of these expensive wines of hers. I was bursting with excitement afterward and barely slept that night.

Around the end of August, I would show up and be paid eight dollars an hour to hand sort each half-ton bin of Pinot Noir grapes before they were destemmed. The sweet, miniature purple fruit was mainly from the Hyde Vineyard down in Napa, but we moved onto some bins of Hirsch Vineyard grapes days afterward that Tasha treated like clustered jewels. A few of Tasha's neighbors turned up to help as well. We worked in the damp rectangular warehouse on her family's property, away from the army of wasps and yellow jackets that buzzed aggressively outside. Tasha's wines were expensive, and now that I was on the production side of the spectrum, I was seeing why they garnered upwards of 40 dollars a bottle. Everything was sanitized with a four part process—if your hands touched the floor or the bottom of a bucket while hand sorting, you had to wash them, but without soap so scented residues wouldn't get into the juice. We were trained to assume that microbial bacteria and bad yeasts were everywhere, and newly crushed grapes were the most vulnerable target. If grapes hit the cellar floor, they were out of the game, no matter how perfect they appeared. Every cluster had to be picture perfect ideal and free of any pink, premature grapes or shriveled, overripe ones. Clusters with mold or raisins were tossed out into the five gallon plastic buckets at our feet, later to be produced into a much heralded and unlabeled "Portuguese Diesel" for local consumption. Six to eight of us would hand sort bin after bin on each side of the destemmer, and I would shyly listen to the local lingo from the hippies at hand.

"I've got mites this year," one woman would say.

"He didn't come home last two nights," said the other. One mustached older guy gave Tasha's nephew the details on how to properly scramble eggs (a recipe I memorized for life: no cream, just a splash of water, salt and white pepper). My coworkers asked each other if they'd seen certain people lately and talked about who got busted for growing marijuana and, always, the weather. My second day, they asked me what my sign was, and when I said "Gemini," the women all nodded their heads and oohed.

On breaks, while I'd sip some dark coffee and take in the expanse of endless wild acres surrounding the warehouse, I'd see some of my colleagues pile into a four-door Honda and hotbox the hell out of it. Tasha never did, so I didn't either. Instead, I badgered her with questions about winemaking and wine in general, and she eagerly answered them all.

The three-hour round-trip commute from Eureka for marginal pay was unrealistic. My wife was probably more lenient than she should've been about it, since we were too broke to afford the gas, but there was no stopping me. I was obsessed.

* * *

After working a second Whitethorn harvest in 2002, I left my wife in June of 2003 on a Greyhound bus bound for my stepbrother's house in Santa Cruz. We had clearly married too young and the naïve enterprise was unraveling at a dangerous, infidelity-driven pace. If I would've stayed in Humboldt County in those prevailing, devastated circumstances, I would've done something foolish and ended up in jail, or, at the very least, clumsily self-inflicted. Broke, crushed, cheated and carless, I boarded that reeking transport full of Pelican Bay excons and Crescent City meth hounds and tied my sole piece of luggage around my ankle for the duration of the trip. Interestingly enough, Tasha stopped crushing wine grapes that year and wouldn't see another bin full of Pinot Noir until 2007 because of relationship issues of her own.

Shortly after arriving in Santa Cruz—by way of the scariest Greyhound station in Northern California (Oakland)—into the open and drunken arms of my stepbrother Tim, I started experiencing violent stomach pains after meals. The pain would build in my esophagus and incinerate the hell out of my upper stomach, the crippling irritation spinning like a hurricane in me for over an hour at times. I soon learned that induced vomiting saved me a lot of time and trouble, and with Tim well accustomed to retching out the previous night's alcohol each morning before work, the routine of puking became nearly a nightly experience. His technique of cutting to the chase and just stuffing three big fingers up his mouth for instant projection worked rather well. This was heavy living (in a converted garage on the gangbanging Eastside, no less).

Was I bulimic now? Or just betrayed? Once Tim used his Cellar Master status to hire me on to Bonny Doon Vineyard's cellar crew, I came to know the stalls of the employee restroom rather well, especially the stained toilet bowl in that haunted garage he let me live in that summer.

A lot of wine drinkers love it when they hear that I worked for eccentric Bonny Doon Vineyard. The wines are world famous for their wild, illustrated label art (by the likes of Ralph Steadman) and off-the-wall names like "Cardinal Zin" and "*Bouteille* Call." People assume that the celebrated owner Randall Grahm and I hung out in a carnival of a wine cellar with midgets, tranny whores in fishnet stockings, clowns doing pump-overs, and some one-eyed hunchback that lived in the barrel room guarding *foudres* of Le Cigare Volant. Aside from a cool week of painting a gritty grey hallway and ceiling the colors of the elements alongside the legendary marketer and *vigneron*, Bonny Doon was a wine factory where you lined up to clock in. It was also the most hostile working environment I'd ever encountered. I was teased for my inexperience, humiliated in Spanish whenever possible, and nearly got jumped on more than one occasion by the familial Latino crew of nine. They had brothers, uncles, and nephews that were frothing for the position I received and probably could've done the job a lot better. I mentioned my concern to Tim and he addressed the issue of a mandatorily friendly working environment at clock-in the following morning in his best ghetto Spanish. This turned out to be a horrible move.

I carried a mallet around in the back of my pants and a pocket full of citric acid for self-defense that day. Something was going down. The guys started things off by calling me homosexual and asking me to do unconstitutional things to their eggs and buttholes—a given. But the main guy harassing me was named Armando and he fired the first bullet when he said "Hola Pelona" to me (which is "hello bald chick," I believe) by the time clock when he returned from lunch. It was mainly a move to impress the female assistant winemaker next to me, who I was helping inventory the yeast and nutrient shipment that had just arrived on pallets. This set me off like nothing had before. My marital stress had certainly taken a toll on my hairline, and I had issues with my increasingly barren forehead. After two weeks of this treatment I'd had enough. I called him a dirty criminal in Spanish and told him he would burn in holy hellfire. (Superstitious threats, I learned, could rile a macho Latino up quicker than cuss words.) Hardcore street Spanish was coherently flowing out of me with accent and ease as we squared off. I remember that 40-year-old cellar worker tripping and going "Huh? Huh?!" as he reached for his knife.

"Fuck you, you criminal!" I yelled in his face, this time in English. I had nothing to lose. No wife. No car. No home. Some temporary job. I was five seconds away from doing the citric-acid-to-his-eyes and mallet-to-his-skull combo that I'd been mentally rehearsing all morning. After all, I had a pocket full of the stuff for a reason. My stepbrother came galloping in and clocked both of us out. He grabbed us both by the arms and told us to leave.

Boiling with anger, I rode my bike along West Cliff Drive on an ironically beautiful afternoon. The ocean was glassy and it hummed its lapping song along the tideline. When I came back to the winery an hour and a half later I was in a mellow daze. The GM told me to clock back in, write up my incident report, and soon that tormentor who'd worked at Bonny Doon for over seven years lost his job.

* * *

October blew its chilly offshore breath into the Doon. I was talking to my wife on a weekly basis via filthy payphones around Capitola. I bought myself a shitty little car and made a mad dash up to Humboldt to give my marriage a second shot. My father had been urging me to work it out, while Tim was wholeheartedly against it. He'd been listening to my sob story on repeat and he too had been betrayed in the past. With only the weekend off from the winery, I pulled a no-show on Monday. The days with my wife at her new place went better than expected, so rather than staying on Highway 101 south to Santa Cruz to clock back in for the seven o'clock night shift, I detoured heavily toward Fort Bragg on the Mendocino Coast and stopped at Pacific Star Winery. Proprietor Sally Ottoson and her partner Bob graciously fed me lasagna with Zinfandel and Anderson Valley Pinot Noir and put me up in their hot tub-adorned guest cabin on the property's cliff. They knew me as a wine writer that praised their Petite Sirah in a story once for *Vine Times magazine*. I drank their B-Bar X Zin under the stars by myself, amazed that I didn't have a stomach flare up.

I didn't call in to Bonny Doon till Tuesday afternoon. I was let go that evening when I finally made it back to Santa Cruz. Since I was the first temp they brought on for the season, they were going to cut me a week from then anyhow since harvest was done, so it was fair enough. Tim was embarrassed and, with malt liquor-scented tears, told me not to speak to him for a couple weeks. He locked me out of the converted garage, so I ended up sleeping at the house on the Santa Cruz harbor that Bonny Doon rented for the international harvest interns. The Australian, Mark, brought home my three gallon carboy of Syrah that I'd made at the winery, which I loaded into my car. With the help of Tim's roommate Zack, I finally got into the garage to get my wine stash and the rest of my clothing.

A surprise and unemployed follow-up trip to my wife's cabin in Humboldt that week proved that things weren't going to work out after all. There was somebody in her house when I called her from the mall in Eureka around 11 p.m. and said "Guess where I'm at right now?" Her sugar-coated long distance tone turned to local black coffee as she realized I was serious. This was the lowest point in my life. I spent three days and nights at her place, hanging out with our dogs, trying not to snoop around the drawers or follow her into town, which she made easy by locking the gate on the property when she'd leave for work. I wrote an emo ballad on the guitar. I drank through a case of samples that got sent to me for some article on Zinfandel that would never be written. She said she needed space and didn't want me just yet. I accused her of seeing the same guy and lying. It was an endless, torturous circle. She called her mother and asked her to please rent me her spare room in Pismo Beach while we worked things out. "You're sending your husband to live with your mother," I said, making sure to repeat that statement.

I found myself sobbing and descending a wooded ridge in Humboldt County with my life and a three-gallon carboy of Syrah going through malolactic fermentation packed into the backseat of my purple Geo Prizm. I really did consider flooring it off the slope. I'm pretty sure that qualifies as having the blues.

CHAPTER 3

I gave myself all day to get to my interview and tour of David Hirsch's vineyard on the Sonoma Coast. Driving west on River Road with a hand-drawn map, I passed through Guerneville and took a right on the Cazadero Highway. I stopped at a bakery in the creekside town of Cazadero itself, thinking I was right around the corner from the vineyard and that this could be my café of choice. The red-eyed and pony-tailed guy in an apron asked in earnest how my day was going and what I was up to.

"Oh, I'm gonna check out the Hirsch vineyard and see if I'm gonna be workin' the wine harvest out there," I told him.

His face beamed with excitement about that. "Oh good. Good. Good luck to you. Maybe we'll be neighbors."

Then I maneuvered the vicious concrete stream of Fort Ross Road, with a hundred switchbacks to its name and no railings to keep you from sailing off to an unfortunate conclusion. I took it slow while a few monster trucks rushed at me from around the curves, nearly reducing me to scrap metal. Finally, I made it to Bohan Dillon Road, which my map told me was the starting point for the last five-and-a half miles of the journey. I set my odometer and crossed a lineup of mailboxes and a few single-lane bridges before dipping down through some dense jungle terrain. This was followed by the steepest incline my Toyota Tacoma had ever encountered. The dirt road became a roller coaster that looked like a giant, dusty "S" up the face of a planet. At one point, the nose of my truck pointed straight to the sky.

After hitting the mountaintop and passing some cows, sheep, and vineyards on the unpaved trail, I found the unmarked winery where the dirt road forked—a dark, wood-paneled building, lined with redwood trees semi-sunken into the earth. I didn't see anyone around this building or near the modular homes to the west. The two barns to the left looked empty as well, so I continued on.

Bohan Dillon Road became a downward slope through vines and a row of chestnut trees, with nothing but heavy redwood forest lining the perimeter, the wooded hillsides dizzying to look at.

To the north the sun shone on an odd sight—two huge, golden domes on a mountaintop. I passed a young-looking Mexican guy in one section of the vineyard, comically stuffing the vigorous grape leaf canopy into the trellis wires. It was hotter than I expected it to be on the Sonoma Coast.

At another split in the road where a red tractor was parked, I followed the directions to the Hirsch residence and headed right down a curvy path with a steep drop off to the east. Another vineyard planting popped into view, and soon some deer fencing appeared on my left. I noticed the three buildings sketched onto the faxed map, and turned in at the gate, parking down in front of a modest, single level brown house and its granny unit.

I stepped out into the sun, followed the stony steps down to a deck, and came up to a sliding glass door. Two cats darted past me. I knocked lightly at first, waited, knocked again, then gave it a bit more force the third time around, all to no avail. It was unbelievably silent out here. Laundry was drying on a clothesline. I called the number on the map and got the Hirsch's answering machine.

I drove back up to the winery. Once I parked in front and rechecked the map, I saw the circle marks around the winery and the tiny words "Meet at winery." At three p.m. exactly, I opened up the outer door to the winery, walked down a few steps, and opened a door on the right and entered a combination office and laboratory. There was an older woman sitting in front of a computer. Civilization existed up here on the mountain, complete with glass beakers and an all-in-one copier. I asked if she was Marie for some reason, having forgotten what David's wife looked like in four month's time.

"No, I'm Marcia," she said, and I walked over and shook her hand.

"I'm Darren. I'm here to see David," I said.

"Oh alright." She got on the office line and called him. "Hi... hi David? It's Marcia. Darren's up here to meet with you?" A pause. "Okay." She hung up. "He'll be up in a few." The office went silent then as she looked at me. I tried to engage her in the meantime with some small talk, but it wasn't too well received. She just sort of stared at me. Finally, I heard the door behind me open up and, appearing in a ripped, pale blue button-up shirt, jeans, boots, and a straw hat, was David.

"I'm David Hirsch," he said with a smirk and shake of the hand.

* * *

Getting into David's big truck for a tour through the vineyard, I flatlandishly put on my seatbelt. David heard the click, looked over at me, and said, "No no, you won't be needing that." I unbuckled and leaned back. He fired up his Dodge and we slowly bounced up into a section of his property to see some of the newer vineyard plantings. He talked about the land in an old-timey, nearly mythical narration, citing the history of sheep ranching in the area, the seismic activity, and the lumber barons who had cleared the redwoods years ago. He'd stop talking and look at me and my lips to gauge my reaction to what he was saying. I was following him the best I could as he talked about clones of Pinot Noir and blocks and philosophy.

"There are twenty-five different vineyards up here," he said about his operation. Then he pointed out the neighboring vineyards in view—Marcassin Blue Slide Ridge, W.H. Smith, Failla, Peay, Silver Oak, and Pahlmeyer. This was it. This was the place to grow expensive, wild Pinot Noir, and he was the pioneer from the Bronx that did it first.

"What are those gold domes over that way?"

"Oh, that's Odiyan, the Buddhist center. It's a retreat."

We pulled up to a spot of land ripped apart by constant activity from the San Andreas Fault, which ran right through his land. He explained that this variation of soil types required him to plant Pinot Noir onto different rootstocks that were engineered to handle the demands of the earth. One hillside would be too fertile, so the Pinot was planted onto a stressing root selection, whereas another ridge was all rock and no dirt, so a vigorous rootstock was being used. We parked and stepped out onto the dirt. I took photos while David stuffed the stragglers from the leaf canopy up into the trellising wires. I saw the green, developing fruit and took a picture of him talking about the vines. In the eastern distance lay the golden, dry hills of interior Sonoma County dotted with oak trees and the occasional country home.

"I'd love to be a part of this, David," I said.

"Oh yeah, it's great," he mentioned proudly. "I wish Mick was up here to meet you and talk to you about the job. He's a good winemaker."

Back at the winery, he walked me to a trailer-like modular home with a small fence circling it. I'd share that living space with Mick if I chose to work there. It was a big rectangle with a sliding glass door and a couple huge redwood trees swaying above it. He didn't have a key to show me inside, but I looked in and saw a couch and a little kitchenette. Seemed good enough for me.

We walked back across Bohan Dillon Road and entered the cellar, which was roaring with the sound of humidifying misters and fans running full blast. 60 barrels or so were arranged in rows and stacked four barrels high on racks. David grabbed a couple wineglasses and what looked like a glass turkey baster. He found a particular barrel, removed the silicone bung, and siphoned out a couple tastes from the previous growing year. With that first scent, I was sold on the job. I'd tried a lot of Pinot Noirs at this stage in my life, since San Luis Obispo had three great nearby regions that specialized in the varietal, but none of them compared to the quality of David Hirsch's. To be growing grapes this far out in the middle of nowhere, let alone build a multi-million dollar winery on the ridge to craft your own estate wine, bordered on insanity. This barrel sample screamed world-class Pinot Noir from the first huff — carrying a rich, raspberry perfume and loaded with thick cherry flavors, orange peel and maple syrup spice.

After sampling four different Pinots, he told me there was a wine event coming up at Fort Mason in San Francisco called Pinot Days, and he suggested that I come up for it so I could meet Mick and taste around the venue. My mind was reeling from the tour and the tastes. Here I was with an opportunity to live in the country and be a part of one of the most famous vineyards in the world.

David walked me to my truck and I gave him a bottle of Pinot Noir from one of the best central coast vineyards (though it would taste like rosé in comparison). "Thanks for showing me around," I said with a handshake.

"I hope this all works out," he smiled.

I hit the dirt road to the city, excitedly clenching the wheel with the unprecedented, wild path my life was about to take. We didn't discuss pay, benefits, or anything. All I knew was this was an experience I couldn't miss.

CHAPTER 4

I entered my 31st year in flames. My acid reflux was in fine form and the indicators were making themselves known that third week in June, complete with two bouts of vomiting. Quitting caffeine for a pitiful two days, I suffered through the nagging, sore-headed withdrawals and ultimately fell off that wagon on my birthday itself, drinking a cappuccino and smoking weed on the way to the beach with my surfing friend Alex, only to feel the fire in my throat as we paddled out to some fairly heavy surf. My stomach pounded against my board and sparked a smokestack inside. I've experienced heartburn in the ocean for years, but this was more intense. Somehow I thrived amid the aggravation, and with the waves and ocean conditions being good, I tucked into three long tube rides along the way. As I approached the tideline with hot, aching hiccups, I knew I was in for a serious stomach storm.

Walking up the beach toward the campground where we were parked, I cursed myself as the waves were still going off around us. There would be no second session. Strange spicy belches were a given. I had a doctor's appointment in three days, but knew that wasn't going to be soon enough. It was a crime to cut this daytrip short because of my health, especially since the surf at Jalama Beach was usually windblown and messy by 11 a.m. this time of year.

As I pulled out of the day use parking area for our premature trip home, I got the spits, which is usually my drug-like euphoric relief when it comes to my stomach condition. Sucking the digestive juices down merrily and thinking the pain was over, I jokingly announced to Alex, "I'm ready for another double capp." He was wearing my beanie and widening his eyes at the pain I was experiencing. Being a good ten years younger than me, this Pismo Beach grommet that I'd been taking on surf trips now and then had never seen a grown man in pain. The aching subsided as we drove east on Jalama Road, but momentarily at that. This was going to be a nasty, venomous ride no doubt.

Once in Lompoc, we passed El Taco Loco #2 where I'd usually pull off to eat after surfing and I even gazed at it endearingly, even though I'd told Alex that "a single ketchup packet would land my ass in the hospital."

Passing the donut store on the right, Alex pointed and said "Wouldn't some donuts be good for you right now, Delmore?"

"Check your smart-ass remarks at the door," I told him.

There was a Vons supermarket with a pharmacy attached up ahead. I was going in for Pepto even though I knew they'd be candy at best. Alex still had donuts on the brain, so we reconvened in the parking lot: me with the pink tablets and Alex with a generic powdered dozen. I chewed on a pink trio of tablets and washed the sweet chalky residue down with a sip of water. Alex held up a donut with his blonde, furry eyebrows raised. "Not a chance in hell," I said.

In the corridor between Vandenberg Air Force Base and Orcutt, Alex looked over at me with white donut powder clotted in the corners of his mouth as I hunched over the wheel with a strained, dying expression on my face.

"You're not doing well, are you?"

"Just revel in how well this Grateful Dead song matches the scenery," I advised. It hurt just to listen to someone speak. "And how about wiping the nasty corners of your mouth already?"

I dropped him off in the village of Arroyo Grande in the midday heat, my stomach one nauseated and hellacious mess. The wafting fried food in the wind nearly made me retch as I reversed out of the lot and sped away. Was this spastic colon now? Maybe I had a pinched lower intestine? It felt like some internal organ got clenched up in a vice or clamp along the way.

At home I propped all of my pillows so I could sit upright in bed; lying on my side or my stomach was out of the question. It was strange how it persisted, even after I got the spits for a second time. My stomach was puffed out like a starving Ethiopian's and twitching like there was an alien baby inside. It was an internal battleground, like I'd drunk a Jamba Juice with a battery acid boost.

Shortly after, I induced some vomiting of green bile (think jalapeños with lime powder), and the crippling dry heaves followed. I was laid out on the bathroom floor with my arms wrapped around the toilet bowl. Was this stomach hemorrhaging? I would need my prescription pronto. My roommate, Adam, was home, and he could hear what was going on.

"D, are you dying on me?" he finally asked through the bathroom door.

"Pretty much," I gasped from the floor.

"I have these popsicles in the fridge. Maybe that'll help. And if it doesn't, at least your puke will be more colorful."

"Thanks. I'll try that out."

Adam had seen me suffer at least a dozen times since I'd been renting a room in his house. This was far worse than the time he was on his way out the door to catch a flight at four in the morning and I scared him. I was sitting upright on the living room couch in the dark with my car keys in hand and a jacket on, burping and shaking. I ultimately drove myself to the ER that morning—mostly due to his insistence—and went broke because of it.

I washed my mouth and face before exiting the bathroom. I looked up my doctor's office number in the yellow pages, an exhausting feat in my state of being. Once through to the receptionist, I delivered my plea, got transferred to a different woman and then repeated myself. She asked me which pharmacy I use. Then she said she'd try to call it in before five. It was only three o'clock in the afternoon.

"Try?" I asked. "I'm really in a world of pain here. Do I call you back to check, or…"

"You can call Longs Pharmacy to check on it."

She didn't call it in till five to five.

I walked into Longs in shorts, sandals, and a thick jacket (even though it was 95 degrees out), with my bearded, sweaty face and hair all wild. I was shivering. Judging from the alarmed response of the white-cloaked girl at the pharmacy counter, I had the look of a dying man. She went back to check on the progress.

"Looks like it'll be ten minutes for him to type it up," she said.

Over a hundred bucks later, I left with a month's supply of acid-blocking Protonix pills. In the car I took one without water and drove home, happy to be sitting upright while the pill went down. But this wasn't going to be a miracle worker. Once home, I took a Vicodin and got back into bed. I could sit in the same position for only 20 minutes at a time—that's how the pain traveled.

In the awful blue glow of the living room past midnight, I knew it was time to make that northbound move.

* * *

A week later, after a painful upper endoscopy where what must have been a Betamax-sized camera was stuffed down my throat, I found myself at the Radiology department of a Santa Barbara hospital. The silver-headed radiologist spoke softly to me in the darkened room. With the hum of medical machinery all around us and the hour barely past seven, we were water-cooler talking before getting on with the details of the procedure. My mother's restaurant came up in the course of conversational things. He knew of it, though he hadn't been in to eat for a long time. Soon an unwarranted vein of an affair he had in the mid-1980's was mentally spiked and flowing.

"Let me just put it like this," he offered about his last patronage. "There was a wild storm that night, and the power went out at the restaurant. There were two people sharing a table, candlelight was all that was left, and one of them shouldn't have been there." A fluorescent green glow highlighted his coat and chiseled cheeks while he poetically recounted the lustful eve.

It was premature for a man of my age and physique to be here. After all, I surfed all the time, ate organically and mostly vegetarian, and was within my normal weight category. I didn't touch cigarettes, fast food, hard alcohol, energy drinks, or sodas. I had a fairly easy wine tasting room manager job in the idyllic Edna Valley. I did drink rivers of wine and espresso, and smoked quite a bit of marijuana, but aside from such vices I was more health conscious than any of my friends. But there I was on the second tier of the medical exploration into why I'd landed in the hospital twice in six months with a leaky clamp in my esophagus and pain that made me simply want to die.

"So let me explain to you a little about the process," the radiologist said, emerging from his shady memory lane. "Now, I'm going to spread a little radioactive material on an egg sandwich, or it'll possibly be stirred into some soup from our cafeteria. I will be the one to warn you that if you are accustomed to the cuisine of Wolfgang Puck, you're not necessarily going to be wowed this morning." He snorted at his own straight-faced humor, even as the joke fell on its face. It was early, not a drop of coffee was in me, and I was going broke over these examinations. "But as it gets inside of you—the sandwich that is—we're going to have you lie down on that table beneath the lens over there, and I will read the radioactivity inside you. While it's doing this, I will probably alternate between monitoring you and, hell, having a smoke outside." He paused, and we just stared at each other. I offered a chuckle, but it wasn't a joke; he would smoke about half a pack by the time I was gone. "And using the technology at hand—which I will gladly show you if it's of any interest to you—we will gauge how long it takes for your body to break it down to see if you have what they're now calling 'Lazy Stomach'." He rolled his eyes. "Five years ago it was called 'indigestion.' So," he paused to cross his legs, "do you have any concerns about any of this?"

The notion of digesting nuclear matter wasn't sitting well with me, but then again nothing really was. "No, not really," I said, busy with the visual of melting the toilet at a café afterwards with some fluorescent orange bowel movement.

He stared at me and made some quiet observation. Then he nodded, exhaled through his white-flocked nostrils and left me there with a cigarette-scented pat on my shoulder to fetch the *cuisine du jour*. I looked around and saw some unfathomable equipment, the man's certificates on the wall, a few family photos. I stared at one of him and who I presumed to be his wife, toasting margaritas at a tropical swim-up bar. They looked happy, yet I could only picture that scandalous night he had at my mom's place.

"Puerto Vallarta," he announced from the doorway, sending my pulse to techno.

"Oh, really? Um. Nice. I was there once. For a wedding." I sat back down.

He started preparing the items on a counter behind me before coming around with a grey padded apron. "Okay, I'm going to put some protective armor on you."

The weighted getup Velcro'd around my shoulders and covered what had once been called my "'nads" by an older nurse at a "Doc-in-the-Box" in Arroyo Grande, California. This time, though, the pad was there to protect me from whatever I'd be eating, not the flash of an X-Ray.

"Now, after I wine-and-dine you here," he said with that snort of laughter, "I'm going to have you lie down on your back in the examination room over there—beneath the lens of course—and fall asleep if you want to. They say it takes about three hours to do this properly, but some also say that an accurate reading is available by two hours in. I'll be happy to go the distance if you want to stay the whole way through. But just so you know, this isn't confinement. You wouldn't be hurting my feelings by leaving earlier, if you like."

With a gloved hand he offered me half of a sandwich on a paper towel. "You're in for a treat," he announced. "We have chicken salad today." I examined the suspicious, mayo-heavy specimen that demanded a shield to be worn by the diner. It looked normal enough. I guess I expected to see a bright yellow blob oozing from beneath the bread with the capacity to make the office furniture start sweating. The radiologist suspiciously had a half sandwich of his own on a paper towel, and after removing his glove, he sat down across from me and took a bite.

Chewing and wiping the corner of his mouth, he said, "Now as you can see I've decided to join you here, although my sandwich is not of the nuclear persuasion." He followed that with another bite. "Make sure not to spill any of yours on the floor. If you do, we'll have to neutralize the department entirely."

"Neutralize the department?"

"It's quite the pain in the ass," he said with a snort.

We smacked away at our chicken salad sandwiches in the near dark, me babying it with both hands and nibbling so as not to cause atomic fallout. I nearly lost a few crumbs to the floor while I brainstormed the possible environmental effects of the nuclear marinade. Would it sear my tongue? Would it burn tissue on its way down? Was it killing off a part of me through digestion? I guess these were some of the "concerns" he asked me about that I didn't voice. I just ate the sucker.

The tainted mayo was graciously applied, masking what the wino in me kept trying to detect out of curiosity. I had imagined the atomic spread would taste citrusy, with tart, lemony nuclear acid, almost like a bright, unoaked Chardonnay, but I was just getting the bland diced chicken and the mayonnaise.

"Salt?" he offered. I nodded, and he handed me a little packet. I sprinkled some right on top of the bread and chewed away, each bite beginning the long, aggravated journey down. He put his glove back on and stood. "Well, it wasn't the Four Seasons," he said as he took my paper towel away, "but it'll do."

* * *

After two and a half hours beneath the lens, I learned that it took me 57 minutes to digest half of a sandwich.

"Now I'm no real doctor," he said as I put on my sweatshirt and looked at the computer screen over his shoulder, "but in my experience, I'd say that's slow, but fairly normal. But again, I'm not a real doctor. He'll decide."

I thanked him, invited him back to my mom's restaurant sometime, and left the radiology department wondering what it was that *wasn't* a lazy stomach or an ulcer that caused me such pain when I ate every night. With acid reflux, diet seemed to be everything to some doctors, where to others it was more of a state of mind. I was becoming more and more convinced that it was my divorce and the resultant heartbreak igniting a chain reaction of the two. But relationships dissolve every minute in this world, and I felt alone in my claim that it was all stemming from love gone wrong. Could a person really leave me a lifetime of fiery intestinal pain that was best relieved by stuffing a hand down my throat and purging into restaurant toilets? The bulimic approach was far superior to floundering in internal, all-consuming pain for hours on end after half of a dinner. The results of my upper endoscopy would likely tell all, but I was already starting to believe that a woman was to blame.

CHAPTER 5

At the end of June, I spoke with Mick and David and accepted their offer. I was officially a harvest cellarhand for Hirsch Vineyards, and I made it clear that I was looking for full time work if things went well. David was excited and told me so. Mick, who I had yet to meet, seemed a bit odd on the phone and intense, but liked my experience with Tasha at Whitethorn Winery. The pay wasn't good, but living on the property was included and I'd be able to start in early August to get acquainted with the winery before the grapes ripened. I gave notice at my tasting room job in San Luis Obispo and told Adam I was moving up North. I didn't have many belongings, so moving would be easier than ever before.

In July, I was able to meet Mick in person at Pinot Days San Francisco, which was a tasting event on the pier at Fort Mason featuring wineries that specialized in Pinot Noir. I arrived early with the pass David arranged for me and searched for the Hirsch Vineyards sign. The winery representatives were just setting up. I saw a middle-aged guy with a serious look on his crimson face decanting a bottle of wine by himself. It was definitely the Hirsch table but I kept walking. I circled back after eyeballing the layout of the event and introduced myself. He smiled and, in a distinctly East Coast accent, said, "Darren, good to meet you." David and Marie Hirsch turned up then and the vibe turned jovial. More people were showing up to taste, and David urged Mick to take a half hour to go taste with me. I broke the ice the best I could, but his silence and intensity made it difficult. We started off at the Louis Latour table and tried a few red Burgundies. He would ask me what I thought about each wine, and in a way, this was a second interview. I was honest and didn't get too geeky about each wine. By the time the 30 minutes had passed, we were getting along okay at the Bjornstad Cellars table. He knew a few winemakers from the Sonoma area and I knew a lot of the central coast contingent there. We ended up back at the Hirsch table, which was crowded with tasters. Mick confirmed my start date on the calendar on his phone, then we shook hands and I said bye to David and Marie.

* * *

On August 8th I made my move. Driving out to the vineyard on a warm Sunday afternoon, I opted to bypass Cazadero proper and take the alternate route for a glimpse of the sea. Passing the coastal township of Jenner in a mere ten seconds, I headed north to Meyers Grade Road and cut up the mountain. This seemed like a more self-preserving route than Fort Ross Road. I couldn't get over the beauty and ruggedness of the whole area, with the endless expanse of the ocean to the west and nothing but open hillside to the east. Each parcel of land must have been a minimum of 50 acres. I couldn't accept the realization that I now lived and worked here. Amid the frenzy of moving and driving major freeways with my belongings in the bed of the truck, I was only running on a chocolate croissant and a bag of tortilla chips.

I arrived at the stuffy trailer on the Hirsch Vineyard and immediately set to cleaning; I opened the windows to release the stale air and wiped down just about every portion of my new living space with isopropyl alcohol. Very "micey" was the best way to describe the trailer's bathroom. Once finished, it took me two hours to move my whole life from my truck into the trailer: clothes, food, wine, and guitars. On the electric stove, I put on a pot of pasta (which would surely be met by plenty of self-induced acid in my stomach). I sat down at the little dinner table and snacked on a cracker with a lively glass of Tablas Creek Vermentino.

The thing, be it trailer or modular home, was wood-paneled on the interior, with a little stretch of carpet in the living room complete with a futon, coffee table, and a mini DVD player. There was a laundry-style room in back with a frightening amount of empty glass bottles piled on the chintzy linoleum, mostly of the Lagunitas IPA persuasion.

I got up and walked out on the back porch with my glass of wine. Redwood trees towered around me, the late afternoon sun glowing between them. A silver Landcruiser pulled up and a man in a baseball cap, white T-shirt tucked into jeans, and *botas* popped out and went into the trailer across the way. I figured it was the vineyard intern named Greg that Mick told me about. I pocketed the pipe I'd been smoking and decided to go introduce myself.

Out the front door and down the wood ramp, the man looked at me questionably as I approached him.

"Hey, are you Greg?" I asked. Upon closer sight, this dark, mustached man sitting on his own front steps of a trailer was older and Latino. His big leather belt had a green pot leaf design on it. I walked over past the back end of our side-by-side vehicles to introduce myself.

"*Me llamo Darío,*" I said, having learned at Bonny Doon that "Darren" wasn't the easiest name for a Mexican to pronounce. This seemed to impress him, and I followed it with a textbook, "*Como te llamas?*"

"Rígo," he said.

We had somewhat of an exchange, and in light of this guy's probable drunken state, I was kicking ass *a la Español* already. He mentioned that his family lived in both Guerneville (which he pronounced "Gurr-when-ah-veel") and Modesto, that his older brother worked here on the vineyard, and his friend Julí lived with him in the trailer. Julí soon sauntered out wearing only soccer shorts, a big beer belly protruding over the thin elastic waistband. He looked as if he had just woken up.

I could see now that Rígo was stoned if anything, and he wanted to rap some more. He told Julí that I spoke Spanish well, and kept saying "*dílé*" about me to Julí, which I thought was past tense for "said," though past tense is where I fell off in my foreign language studies. I made a mental note to look that up in my dictionary to ensure they weren't calling me a goat fucker like their brethren did at Bonny Doon.

"*Voy a comer,*" I told Rígo, but instead he started showing me this piece for a car or some type of machinery and asking for my opinion on it. Hailing from a long line of amazingly unskilled male laborers, I couldn't help him there. Instead I asked him "*Tú tocas la guitarra?*" He smiled a bit, tripping on the question. "*No, no. Un poquito, pero no.*"

"*Traigo tres guitarras,*" I told him. I was hoping to have a Calexico-style jam experience up in here, but it looked unlikely. "*Hasta luego,*" I said.

"*Hasta luego.*"

* * *

The view out the back porch of the trailer at sunset was magical. The sky was ablaze in copper, pink and crimson, with a bed of thick gray fog hovering beneath it all. I made myself mosquito proof and took my acoustic out on the back deck to sing some old country songs. It was dead quiet aside from the occasional breeze through the trees and my fingerpicking. I felt good, safe, and at ease.

CHAPTER 6

I slept in my sleeping bag on the futon in the entry room. At around five a.m., a missionary clanging of bells rang out from somewhere, alerting me of my first day of work, but I slept through most of it, thinking it was the whole ranch's alarm clock. Maybe it was the nearby monastery. I drifted off to sleep and had the most bizarre dream that was inspired by the previous evening's phone call to a good winemaking friend in Oregon. He used a raw, funny way to describe me quitting my full time job, leaving my hometown, and moving way out to the Hirsch Vineyard to work the harvest.

"Damn, D, you're just tossing your nuts over your shoulder and going for it, huh?"

I'd never heard that one before and, thanks to the visual it conjured, I had a dream about some guys and myself nakedly jumping off a pier in the night. But before doing so, we had to sling our testicles up over our shoulders before leaping. We all had these grotesque, gravity-weighted stringy long sacks that hung to the soggy, wet pier planks, and up and around our shoulders they went before jumping off. The same dream featured a barn that doubled as a white trash living room and Asian convenience store.

The bells woke me up again. Upon further annoyed investigation at around six, I found it to be Mick's alarm clock from his empty back bedroom. I shut it off and crawled back into my sleeping bag. The smell of exhaust flooded the living room next, the rumbling of a nearby generator going. I heard voices and vehicles starting up.

I submitted to the fact that the ranch was alive and working and got up and brewed a pot of my newest coffee substitute—Rooibos tea—and matched it with a banana and granola eaten out of a mug with "Happy Birthday" emblazoned across it.

Mick's instructions were to meet on the crush pad at seven a.m., where a nearby rancher's wife named Barbara would be waiting for me to start sanitizing hoses for the day's transferring of wine from barrels to tanks. I apprehensively walked across the dirt road toward the winery at five 'til and, upon opening up the cellar door, saw a strong, mulleted figure in jeans sitting on the stairs and reading a manual. As the figure stood in a flower printed shirt and walked over to meet me, I could tell that this was Barbara, and this was Northern California.

"Hey, you must be Darren," she said in a deep, unenthusiastic voice.

"Yeah. Barbara?" We shook hands, and she told me that the pump wasn't working. There was an air leak when you turned it on. She'd called Mick on the cell phone a couple times already and he was going to pick up a new diaphragm on his way out from Napa Valley, assuming it was pierced.

David Hirsch was out and about soon after, and I saw him with his hat on and that torn, blue button-up tucked into his jeans. He waltzed in and happily greeted me as I was sanitizing five glass carboys that would hold the Chardonnay lees from today's racking. He left the cellar, hopped on a forklift, and started moving huge planks of wood around, setting them in a stack on the dirt across from the winery to make room on the outdoor crush pad for the upcoming week of bottling. Barbara and I helped him out for awhile, and then she left us to go tidy up the winery equipment shed.

When Barbara took the hose into the storeroom to spray away the mouse shit, she pulled aside a couple pieces of wood and a snake started grooving its way against the wall.

"David! There's a snake over here!" she shrieked, coming out of the storeroom with her hands up alongside her head. "Oooh, I hate snakes!"

David was handling a cell phone call to a banker while maneuvering and he ended it with a calm, "Look I gotta go; I'm in the middle of a very delicate situation here." He hung up and asked Barbara what kind of snake it was.

"I don't know! It could be a rattler."

"Did it rattle?" David asked with a grin, backing away from the wall on the forklift with a 40-foot long plank of wood spread across the forks. Finally, he set it down and we walked over to where Barbara stood by the outside sink.

"Ooh, it's out here now!" she shouted, backing away from the building. "I started spraying it in there."

I followed David's lead, feeling caffeinated by what could be a heavy scene. I acted ready to help, even though I was secretly terrified. I'd envisioned rattlesnakes all over this property, not to mention mountain lions and bears. The Sonoma Coast was known for great populations of all three. And now one of those dangers was becoming a reality on my first day on the job.

When we finally saw the snake, it was slender and had suspicious markings that could've been those of a juvenile rattlesnake. I'd pictured rattlesnakes to be thick, massive serpents. David grabbed the hose and started spraying it in the face. I did some spastic dance floor moves behind him to help. There was a sanitized five-gallon bucket next to me, so I picked it up.

"You're spraying him into the drain!" Barbara said.

"D'you want me to bucket him?" I ventured to offer, not really sure what "bucket him" would actually entail, but it sounded good. It caught David's attention for a second, and then Barbara grabbed a shovel and smacked that thing good. She chased it away from the wall and out on the crush pad. She was actually running full bore with the thing cradled in the shovel till she scooped it up and tossed it down the hill.

Hopefully the snake solved the mouse problem before the unexpected escort out. I had the aching suspicion that this was only the beginning of what we would encounter from the wild this harvest.

Shortly afterward, we saw Mick approaching us in cargo pants and a tucked in t-shirt, carrying a cardboard box full of supplies and an awfully serious look on his face. I shook his hand but there was a heavy vibe about him; he immediately wanted Barbara to show him the problem with the air pump in the cellar. Assuming the diaphragm was punctured, Mick tore the entire pump apart and put in a new diaphragm. Just as he was sealing it together, David Hirsch came into the barrel room to check on things. He had been out in the vineyard all morning with the crew, and I spotted an earwig on his hat and found myself swatting away at it to help. He took his hat off and said "Hey, bug off!" to it.

He asked Mick if anyone had turned on the air compressor that morning. Barbara looked embarrassed right away and said, "Aw, man. Dad gummit." The pump wasn't the problem at all. The air was never turned on to give it juice. Mick asked Barbara to hold out her hand, palm down, and gave it a Catholic style smack.

"Well, let's get it on and get going with the Chardonnay," David added, sauntering out the cellar door.

I was left alone to sanitize two portable, square-shaped, 500-gallon capacity stainless steel tanks that the Chardonnay would go into. Sanitizing here at Hirsch required a solution of sodium percarbonate (what we would call

"Proxy") for the cleaning, then citric acid for neutralizing the residue that is left behind, followed by a water rinse. This is considered mild by wine industry standards, though a good blast of either of these solutions in the eyes or down the throat could be a serious problem.

Barbara, the vineyard intern Greg (who was a tall, retired, pony-tailed wine collector from Healdsburg), Mick and I were standing around the air pump as we were running the same sanitizing cycle through it, and I found myself foolishly in charge of the on/off control and the PSI knobs. As it ran with the citric acid rapidly pumping through the lines, I confused Mick's direction of "stop" with being ordered to stop the pump, and his second warning of "stop!" with adjusting the PSI, to finally him saying, "No, Darren! Literally, just stop!" with a look of death. I backed away from the pump completely. Mick was frustrated, running an aggravated hand through his spiky, graying hair. I was really thankful that Barbara was around. After that incident, I was told by Mick to get the three-inch valves to put on the big tanks so we could sanitize them. As I nervously scavenged the store room, not finding the aforementioned stainless steel valves, Barbara came in, mentioned that she didn't think we had a three inch valve, then said, "Come on, I'll take the heat for it."

We ended up having to use a steel reducer to clamp onto the one-inch valves that we actually did have and, at last, we were ready to start racking wine around lunchtime.

* * *

I celebrated the end of the first 12-hour workday with a massive, lemon-limey swig of the remaining Vermentino. It was time to break out my soy-ginger-lime marinated tofu and couscous specialty, since I was beaten down after working such a stressful introductory day. Mick obviously assumed that I was more familiar with the machinery and the winemaking methods here than I was. When he interviewed me over the phone a month beforehand, I answered all of his questions honestly and without ego. I'd been a tasting room manager for close to three years and hadn't worked consistently in a cellar since 2004. As far as how it all went, I'd say there were cool moments where we collectively enjoyed ourselves, but a lot of moments where I felt useless, and a time where I saw a demon in the winemaker and even wondered if I would have to bow out. That was on day one. Where was my commitment?

CHAPTER 7

I struggled through a nervous sleep after the first workday. The air mattress that was propped up on the plywood was a strange nest and the discovery of rat droppings on it didn't freshen up the situation by any means. My stomach was full of bubbles and tremors, and I feared the forthcoming shift. You could hear when other people used their toilets—Rígo and Julí were most likely the first. I heard Mick get up and grind some coffee beans. After spending the majority of the night searching for a signal, my fully-charged and mostly unused cell phone died out around four a.m.—and with it, my alarm clock. Mark knocked around 5:30. We were working from six to six; I needed to embrace the early morning work hour, because Barbara told me six a.m. was the start time during bottling and harvest.

Day two turned into a snarling beast. We had a half hour lunch break, finished work at nine p.m., and I got paid $100 for that. The entire day's duties were absurd and dangerous, including barrel lifting from stacks of barrels up three-high, some of it without the forklift. The letters B, C, or M were chalked onto the front of all the barrels full of wine, which stood for three different blends that David had decided on. The B's were reserve wines, the C's were essentially C grade and would become $30 bottles of wine, and the M barrels were from a nearby vineyard called MacDougall. We were only transferring the C's and the M's into tanks, meaning all the B barrels had to be physically moved onto the same barrel racks together in sets of two and forklifted out of the old barrel room and into the new barrel room to age for another six months.

David would pop in from working out in the vineyard to man the forklift. I felt the urge to buy him a new blue button-up every time I saw him. The one he wore everyday made him look like he'd been run over by a tiller.

Our team consisted of Mick, Barbara, Greg, myself, and a guy named Scott who was just helping out for the day. His family owned Point Reyes Vineyards and he was here to get more experience. Mick used an instrument called the Bulldog Pup to suck the wine out of each barrel. This is a device with a stainless steel rod that hooks up to a gas, such as Argon or Nitrogen, to pump wine up out of a barrel without the use of oxygen. The Bulldog Pup sends in gas to displace the wine up into the rod and through the hoses toward the tank. Because of that, there is a lot of intense pressure built up in each barrel and the lines, and there are stories of too much gas being used and the entire wooden circular heads of barrels blasting open and gas and wine going everywhere. Mick had prefaced his use of the Bulldog Pup that morning in terms of possible death or injury before mentioning that he'd be doing that part of the job.

We'd look up at him from the cellar floor as if he was a god, and Greg, Scott and I would attempt to fill the awkward silence with wine questions for Mick. Sometimes it was cool, like when his sommelier background got him excitedly talking about wine, but when Mick got sidetracked and sediment from the bottom of the barrel would start to go in the line, he'd snap and swear, and the small talk was over. "Fuck!" he'd scream right there in front of Barbara. Our end of the deal was to physically lift down the empty barrels and move them outside to wash. David insisted that we save whatever sediment remained and dump it into this long plastic tank that was outside.

"This place is always a clusterfuck," Scott said to me during one of the more hectic moments. Getting the B barrels onto the same racks once the C's were emptied was a mission. I liked it when Scott and Greg were around; it wasn't until they left and it was simply Barbara and I there to clean up that Mick showed his irritation and started shouting at us again. By the time all the C grade wines had been transferred into the two largest stainless steel tanks in the new barrel room, even David Hirsch was probably in bed.

Mick made a big, respirator-less, sulfites addition in the form of a couple 2.9 liter hits of the powerful preservative. I was standing below him, stabilizing the ladder leading up to the manholes on the tops of each tank, breathing through my shirt with my eyes on fire. I was turning out to be really sensitive to sodium percarbonate, let alone potassium metabisulfite. The fresh mixture of proxy Mick had me mix up for the next day's work was burning my eyes and nostrils. I'd worked with far harsher chemicals at Bonny Doon and Eberle, so it caught me off guard. Mick said it was strange since proxy was the most environmentally friendly cleaning agent for a winery.

"It's essentially hydrogen peroxide," he pointed out. I found myself stupidly using my t-shirt to dab away my tearing eyes, which resulted in even more burning.

Back in the trailer, I took a long shower. As I dried off, I noticed the athlete's foot ointment and spray on the sink. I looked down at my own feet and quickly slid on my dirty socks. After changing, I cooked some soup and grilled a sandwich in the empty trailer, semi-relaxing and reading Henry Miller's *Big Sur and the Oranges of Hieronymus Bosch* at the table. Mick and his giant wolf dog Cornelius came in. As Mick showered, Cornelius circled me like a great white shark, occasionally pausing to sniff my plate. Mick emerged with these big, airy, rubber sandals on his feet. I cringed at that, wondering if I'd contracted my first bout of foot fungus in our communal shower.

He offered a plastic lab bottle full of Bohan Dillon Pinot Noir that we all labored our asses over. In turn I gave Mick a bowl of the soup I made and he dug it, sitting on the futon with a copy of *Wine Business Monthly* spread out across his lap. We drank our big glasses of fresh wine in silence. At around 10:30, he came over to the table with tired eyes and formally announced, "Thank you for the soup. I am off to bed now. Sleep well."

I stayed up for a half hour more, until Miller's self righteous words looked like big, blurry boxes on the pages.

* * *

The next day presented plenty more incomprehensible challenges. David was worried that the C grade wasn't blended properly and that the common practice of blending a full tank of wine by sparging it with Nitrogen to circulate it (a blender effect) wouldn't suffice. Plus, there were more C grade barrels that he wanted to add to the Bohan Dillon blend and the only tanks we had were already full. Mick informed Barbara and I that we would be barreling down Pinot Noir from each tank to make space for the remaining C grade barrels to join the party. He was not thrilled, and the crazy, fixed smile with which he spoke was disturbing.

Mick was on a serious mission in regards to this new hiccup in the plan. At close to 12:30, he reluctantly told Barbara and I to *go eat*; not *go break for lunch*, but go eat something and return. I walked back to the trailer to heat up some tofu couscous and heard pounding footsteps approaching. Through the kitchen window I saw Mick power walking in his same grey cargo pants and tucked in t-shirt toward the trailer with a bloodshot face most commonly associated with constipation. I pulled my lukewarm lunch out of the microwave and sat down at the table right as he slammed through the front door. I looked up at him and he just stared at me wordlessly. He rushed into the kitchen, yanked open the freezer door, and three huge blue ice cooler packs dislodged and pelted his shins.

"Aw fuck!" he roared.

Asking him if he was okay was out of the question.

"Goddammit!" he screamed, picking them up off the floor and hurling them back into the freezer.

With my stomach condition, I tried to digest so slowly and carefully, with the vibe coming on like amplified distortion. He ripped open a frozen something and chucked it in the microwave. With only 30 seconds on it max, he pulled his lunch out and stood in the kitchen, grinding the half frozen entrée like a wild animal. A minute later, he threw what was left in the trash and charged right out the front door.

"I don't think I'm going to make it," I said out loud, sitting at that table by myself. It was going to be another 13-hour day at least.

Sure enough, it was a long afternoon full of hassles, the main one being the surprise barrel that was randomly full of whole grapes. Normally grape skins are left behind right after fermentation during the pressing process, but a substantial amount of them slinked by into this barrel and clogged Mick's Bulldog Pup. This caused the whole racking operation to shut down for an hour, with straining of wine in the line, then pushing the hose clean with gas and water, all to blast out buckets full of last year's Pinot Noir grapes that made it into a barrel of Pommard clone. He pulled Barbara aside and demanded to know how grapes ended up in the barrel last harvest, but she couldn't remember. Since David Hirsch was playing the purist and didn't filter his wines before bottling, the last thing he and our customers wanted was a whole grape in their glass.

Mick screamed at me to go get a few items out of the toolbox by name and numerical sizing. Being the unhandy son of restaurateurs that I am, I found myself in the storeroom on my knees rifling through what might as well have been an untranslated copy of *The Tibetan Book of the Dead*.

I heard his footsteps pounding my way after a couple minutes and he shouted, "Darren! What are you doing?"

"I'm uh, looking for the—"

"Stop! Move!"

I moved clear out of his way and let him rip through the red toolbox.

Mick showed his strengths and twist-tied copper mesh around the tip of the Bulldog Pup wand as a screen and got the remaining wine out of the barrel. I thought he'd surely want to kill us all, but he handled it so well, even after that raging, minute-long lunch break. He told me to chalk the barrel with the word "grapes." The situation was lightening up, so I asked him, as I chalked the head of the barrel, if I should write *fucking* grapes" instead. But as I was making the joke and writing the word "grapes" much bigger than required, Mick came back with, "You don't have to write it so big that it takes up the whole barrel." We all had a laugh. Then came the welcome news that we were finishing up at six p.m.

With all the hang-ups, I stepped into the office on my way out and asked Mick if he liked falafels. He confirmed it, so I told him he had one coming his way. When I walked over to the trailer I discovered that the front door handle was locked for the second time that day, so I returned for Mick's keys. "Again? Really?" he asked me.

"I've been leaving it open," I said.

"Well, I didn't lock it." He was running some basic lab tests on samples from the blended tanks of wine in the small lab section of the office. He shakily handed over his keys and I went back to the trailer.

As the falafel powder thickened in water, Mick sat on the front porch reading *Wine Business Monthly* with Cornelius while I strummed quietly on the back porch and drank a strange Domaine Roulot Monthélie, thinking the wine was experiencing what connoisseurs call a "closed phase" or was just really French and therefore lighter and different than most California Pinot Noir. Sniffing the cork during dinner later really confirmed that the odd moving mold called TCA was present on this cork and had flawed the wine, and oddly enough, aside from the tell-all chlorinated smell, I realized that the monster garlic I'd bought at the health food store smelled just like it. Mick and I both got halfway through the bottle before I proclaimed that it was corked. "Can garlic be corked too?" I asked him, mentioning the same smells of this wine in the cloves I was using. Mick agreed that the wine was corked, "but very slightly at that." I had a bottle of Pikes Dry Riesling from Australia in the refrigerator as back up, and I offered Mick a glass.

"Ah! The Polish River Valley!" he announced from memory when I mentioned the wine's Clare Valley origin. His passion for wine and years of restaurant work in upper end East Coast restaurants afforded him a heavy knowledge of the world's wines. The Pikes Riesling had tons of citrus on the finish. Mick told me how some wineries actually make a citric acid addition to a white wine before bottling to achieve those lemon and lime acid notes when they're naturally not there.

"This is a lot of fun," he said with a nod and another sip of it, making his way over to the futon in the living room. Cornelius hopped up next to him. The public station KZYX out of Philo was tuned in on his little radio by the door.

I read more Henry Miller at the table post falafel. A lot of the book was about the mysterious X factor, and how an artistic man must either make his living on the side or practice his art on the side. He wrote a lot about geniuses in Big Sur (including himself in that bracket, no doubt) that adopted ordinary, honest working existences, explaining how it was the best way to live.

Mick stood by the dining table after tossing his trash and announced, "Thank you very much for dinner. I will now put myself to bed." He was done.

As his door closed, I had to say that day was the best day I'd performed at the winery thus far. From filling 38 barrels of Pinot out of the tank with no major volcano-like spills, to sanitizing everything right, to laying low at appropriate high-stress moments and offering to do the right tasks at the right times, I pulled it off. Mick was intense with his animalistic work persona, but I was seeing him handle some hellish curveballs in the cellar, and he seemed to know his wines. I just prayed he would never snap on me harder than he had already.

CHAPTER 8

Day four turned out to be the most negative day of them all. Mick really had zero patience. Having to ask him anything a second time was received by a declaration of war. He was under a heavy amount of pressure and releasing his aggression on Barbara and me with ease. He'd yell, give a disgusted look, and be as short with us as possible. Funny how at the beginning of the week, as I'd pass by his truck on the way to the trailer for lunch, I was saying sappy shit to his tied up dog like "Hi Cornelius, your daddy will be coming by soon." Cut to today's classic: "Fuck you, Cornelius." I could've easily urinated on his Alaskan mane around five p.m. to get back at that mean daddy of his. David had promised me that Mick was a patient teacher, and I wondered how a man who was clenching his fists at me painted such a picture.

I had come to the conclusion during the last hour of work that I would be quitting. I took a walk down Bohan Dillon Road to block four with my cell and called Rob in Oregon. All the while I felt strange eyes, or, more frightfully, Mick's, watching me. I kept expecting to see him pop up out of the Mount Eden block and catch me formulating an escape plan. It was very possible that David may have installed vineyard cams out there. At first, I couldn't even get reception, which seemed straight out of a horror movie. Add in an approaching band of zombie Mexicans and David Hirsch on a supernatural tractor above them and you'd have a late-night fright flick on your hands. Was I trapped? Would my truck start in a pinch?

I hated to make Rob and his Oregon job offer a consolation, but it sure sounded great during the last two hours of work where I felt useless, resented, and more of an irritant to Mick than sodium percarbonate in the eyes. And I was doing pretty well all day too.

The night before, Mick had mentioned that last year's intern quit by September 1st. Some guy out of UC Davis moved here around June and gave it a shot for a few months. On Labor Day weekend, right before the picking began, he packed up when Mick was gone, drove up to David in one of the vineyard blocks with all of his belongings in his truck and told him he wasn't having any fun. It made me wonder if there was a recurring theme here.

It would be a shame to quit, but it'd be a bigger shame to be walking around on eggshells and stressed out for the equivalent of five dollars an hour for the next three months of my life. I didn't drop a steady job to move up here and be treated like I was an idiot—stomach condition or not. I felt fooled, tricked almost. Here I was looking for healing in a peaceful agrarian lifestyle, and I'd found the polar opposite in this working environment.

On the phone, Rob relayed some advice from his dad about knowing your place and role, knowing when and when not to speak, and keeping your head down. He laughed at my hippie ideal of everyone getting to know and respect each other at the workplace, and told me to give Hirsch a second week. If that didn't work, David would still have enough time before the grapes came in to find a replacement without any hard feelings.

I walked back to the trailer and found the handle locked again. This was the third time. Mick and I had made a point of keeping it unlocked until I had my own key for it, and I was keeping it unlocked after lunch, only to get off every day to find it locked again. I reluctantly walked over to the winery and found Mick in front of his computer.

"It's locked again," I said.

"Really?"

"Yeah. I left it unlocked at lunch too."

"I haven't been over there."

"Well, someone is obviously going into our trailer."

He handed me his keys, and I went over and unlocked the door, ducking the two hornets that had been buzzing around the doorframe all week long. Once inside the stuffy beast, I tossed the keys on the coffee table and took a long shower. Afterward I started to make some food in the kitchen. Through the window I saw Mick walking over with a clamped jaw. The front door slammed open and he swooped up his keys shouting, "Keys, please!" before charging back to the winery.

"That was nice of him to stop by," I said aloud.

With a plate full of food, I booked it down the hall and locked myself in the rat cage. I was eating and drinking a glass of Melville on the air mattress, watching *Annie Hall* on my laptop and trying to forget the day. Propping myself up on that deflating bed was like navigating a raft down a creek. I decided that dodging Mick for the night might help things out a bit between us. Now that all of the wines (with the exception of the top estate wine) had been successfully racked into tanks for the big bottling that was coming up, I wondered what Friday would have in store for me. I vowed to follow the advice Rob had relayed on the phone about using your eyes and mouth and something about whatever the fuck connects the two.

I passed out early with a dirty Riedel, plate and a fork scattered around me.

CHAPTER 9

I wearily threw on my work clothes after hearing Mick's coffee grinder roar to life. All night long I kept waking up, anxiously listening for the whir of the beans. I couldn't depend on the phone alarm with its dying battery, and I didn't have a clock yet. Judging from the brighter fog outside, it was well past six by now. We must've been starting at seven instead of six, which would've been nice to know.

"Good morning," I said as I walked into the living area. Mick just looked at me while waiting for his coffee to finish brewing and said nothing. Then he sat down on the couch and listened to NPR. I had my cup of granola at the kitchen table while my water boiled. Cornelius came over and put his mouth centimeters from my bowl. I pushed him away. To desperately fill the tense air, I asked, "Anything new on that bridge collapse in the Midwest?"

"There are only eight missing now," he said, holding a green plastic coffee cup as he sat with his legs crossed on the futon. I bypassed the Rooibos tea and made a press of coffee. NPR announced that it was eleven minutes to seven. I went to my room and started putting some things together for a weekend trip down to see Trevor in Petaluma. It looked like I was raring to split, which was partly true. I figured it would be good to call some friends and get a little advice on the matter before I made such a rash decision.

"What's the plan of attack today?" I asked Mick in as optimistic of a voice as I could muster.

He looked down and said, "Oh, gas barrels, put barrels away, pressure wash the floor, clean up after the welder—that kind of stuff." I stepped out the door ahead of Mick for the first time, toward what sounded like a mellow day in viticultural paradise. Man was I wrong.

I've used a pressure washer before, but it had been four years, and as I delicately pushed the blue industrial machine into the cellar, Mick started in with the barking.

"Stop!" he shouted at me. Apparently, it looked like I had the pressure washer plugged in and was moving it a great distance, but it was in fact a different cable that was in the outlet. "Never, *never* move anything that is connected to an outlet!" I did foolishly try to start the pressure washer up inside the cellar, which got his immediate attention. "Stop!" He stormed over to me and told me to hold out my hand for a slapping. "This thing burns diesel! Park it outside!"

After putting on rain boots, fueling the washer up and plugging it into the outside power source, I was off and running, spraying off the black streaks of mold on the cellar walls and ceiling. As I was halfway through blasting with 180-degree water, the rifle I was using disconnected and high pressure liquid heat fried my arm and stomach. The burns set in immediately, and I just dropped everything and screamed. I saw a bacon-like pink color bubbling up on my arm. I ran to a water source and hosed down my stomach with cold water. Mick was working on the paperwork of the week's wine transfers in the adjoining storeroom. Rather than bother him by mentioning I'd scalded the hell out of myself or fill out some kind of accident report, I stubbornly reconnected the gun and picked back up on the task. Ten minutes later he walked through the cellar to find me absolutely drenched and frazzled.

"You know you could wear a raincoat if you want."

Thoughts raged in my head. "I'm soaked because the gun blew off and I got burned." I showed him the arm and the stomach burns. His face grew withdrawn as he recognized the red marks.

"I'm sorry," he said in a doped up way. "I'm sorry."

"Does Barbara have any of that burn cream left?" I asked.

"I don't know. Why don't you ask her?" He returned to his paperwork, annoyed with me all over again.

Barbara was almost happy in a way that the rifle had blasted off on me, because it had happened to her with more severity a month beforehand, and Mick dismissed it as just a Barbara thing. She gave me some burn cream and showed me the remains of her own burns, which looked like a huge birthmark on her right arm.

"Jesus!" I exclaimed.

"It's not that bad anymore," she said.

Mick came up to us with an irritable scowl. "Alright, here's what needs to happen to get out of here today. We need to gas the empty barrels on the crush pad and stack. We have to gas the plastic tanks. We gotta finish pressure washing the old barrel room—"

"You really think he oughta do that?" Barbara chimed in.

He scratched the back of his head and said, "Why? Do you want to red tag the pressure washer now?"

"I sorta think we should," she said.

"All right!" he shouted. "The pressure washer is out of commission." He fired off a number of other jobs to be completed and walked away.

Barbara and I began working on the rest of the tasks, which included disconnecting the faulty part of the pressure washer rifle and boxing it up for him to UPS back to the manufacturer. We tied a tarp over some bottling equipment that Mick used to cork a case of barrel samples for David, then carefully forklifted a pallet of five-gallon glass carboys of leftover Pinot and Chardonnay over uneven ground to the new barrel room.

Around three in the afternoon, David rolled up to see what was happening. I thought about mentioning the burns to him, but he was covered in a layer of brown dirt himself after working in the hot vineyards. Barbara reminded him how she had to get going to make her famous beans for the annual Coyote Picnic, which was a barbecue for all the surviving sheep farmers in the area. Lamb meat was more of an industry than wine grapes in these hills at one time. David told me about the nature of the celebration and how the soaring coyote population literally snacked up the once profitable industry on the Sonoma Coast. The Coyote Picnic began as a weeklong, hard alcohol-fueled binge of these ranchers opening fire on the predators to preserve their industry. In the end, the coyotes won and most of the sheep were devoured, but the picnic and a few of its originators lived on.

"There aren't many of these guys around anymore," David said with raised eyebrows, "in case you want to go." He turned to Mick. "Are you goin' to Barbara's thing? The Coyote Picnic?"

"I plan on sleeping all weekend," Mick said, following it up with some uncomfortable laughter.

Near the end of the day, I stupidly wheeled the full argon tank from the new barrel room to the old one off a single step by myself. I flailed it, and the cylinder snapped out of the bungee securing it to the handcart and smashed into the cellar floor. I'd heard that sometimes those things can take off like a fucking space shuttle when that happens, so I leapt out of the room. Luckily it didn't launch, and Mick didn't see that one. I stood the cylinder back up and strapped it into the handcart, wheeling it over to gas an eighth of an inch of space in a 500-gallon plastic container that held sediment from the barrels of Pinot Noir that we racked. As the gas blew in, most of it splashed right back up at me and onto the floor. I rolled the argon tank back into the storeroom, locked up the back and turned out the light, then headed over to the trailer.

I showered and finished packing for the weekend. As I loaded some things into my truck, Mick and Cornelius strode violently over. He seemed as eager to leave the property for a couple days as I was. After all, bottling and harvest were both looming on the horizon. "Did everything look all right in there?" I said.

"Everything looked great," he said, sounding positive. He rushed into the trailer.

"I'm gonna try to get some waves this weekend."

"That's great," he said in presidential fashion before hopping in his truck. He pulled up closer to the front porch, left the engine roared up and running, and got a few more things out of the trailer. We crossed paths again before he jumped into the truck without a "bye" or a "see ya" or anything, as if he needed to evacuate more than I did.

CHAPTER 10

I don't think Trevor's trashy bachelor apartment was the most serene, uplifting place to spend my weekend. However, Petaluma was the closest and most obvious choice for fleeing the ranch and all it entailed. Trevor had heard me out the night before and advised me to head down, get some surf, and "drink some epic wines, bro."

While driving down 101, I depressurized most of my aggression on the phone to Mary, a girl I'd been seeing off and on for three years. Being an aspiring winemaker herself, she replied to each rant with, "That's not good." She'd worked for some erratic personalities in the wine world already, so her advice was important to me. As I rambled on I kept checking myself, wondering if I was blowing this out of proportion and if I was just a cellar pansy. I questioned if the winemaker I worked for at Eberle Winery who, back in 2004, tried to let me go by telling me I was just too mellow, was actually right. Mary didn't like my plan B of bailing to Oregon, which Rob had confirmed as a real possibility before I called her.

"Darren," he'd said, "I can guarantee you ten an hour and a shitload of overtime, and my boss is one of them bosses who actually wants you to get rich. You know what I mean? You're making five hundred a week now, up here you'll be making seven hundred a week, and you know about the harvest bonus I got last year. But the only bad thing is I work for a redneck who's big and intimidating until you get to know him and see that he's a big teddy bear, just a big teddy bear. And you can drink beer and whiskey and smoke cigs and womanize and get so drunk you fall face down in the dirt, but don't you dare break out a joint. Weed is drugs up here."

Mary cautioned my excitement about this. "Yeah, but I could see you getting a little too smoky up there, though." She was probably right. I could disappear in Oregon. When I first met Mary back in 2004, she was a 21-year-old Cal Poly girl with a tongue ring, motorcycle, and a sizable tolerance for drinking and smoking weed. And even then she was more mature than me. I was playing a heavy rendition of the heartbroken victim of divorce then, which ruined any chance of us having a deeper relationship than what it ended up being. What was surprising was how we maintained some kind of a friendship through the years. Just before moving to Cazadero we had started sleeping together again.

Before getting off the phone with her, she mentioned it wouldn't be a bad idea to go get my burns looked at. I checked the bubbles on my arm and told her I might.

As I pulled up to Trevor's parents' house in Petaluma shortly after five on that warm Friday evening, I found the self-employed individual lying on the couch in trunks and a wife beater in the separated unit his parents had begrudgingly allowed him to live in since his own relationship fallout of 2003. A baseball game was on his dusty box of a television. "Are you ready for some piss and vinegar?" I said as I walked through the door with my backpack.

"Uh-oh," Trevor said, getting up and grabbing me a wine glass. There were dirty dishes on the countertop and in his sink, and a certain reek of fermenting garbage that needed to be taken out. I glanced at the variety of bottles on the chair-less kitchen table and noted that their quality was noticeably lower than those consumed there when he'd dated a cool girl from Siduri Winery. Being the "independent wine broker" that he was, he had on hand a hodgepodge of questionably-acquired samples from a random array of producers. "Off the beaten track" was pushing it as a descriptor of the wineries he represented, but probably the only niche saving his custom Xeroxed portfolio that he was presenting to wine buyers in the North Bay. "Custom Crushed all to Hell," or "One Vintage Away from Bankruptcy" would've been more appropriate categories. He poured me a Tempranillo from Fresno that smelled like shoe polish and tasted like it too.

"You're gonna meet Leslie tonight," he said with his brows raised. "She's got a good palate."

"Leslie? What happened to Grace?" I asked him. He'd been bragging about this nymphomaniac girl he met in an evening class named Grace.

"Oh, she's still on the scene," he clarified with a semi-worried look on his face.

* * *

The next day we ended up going on a wave hunt down through San Francisco and into Santa Cruz. Trevor and I screwed around at a sidewave spot and got a few rides, but nothing inspiring. We cruised around downtown and went into Soif wine shop. I bought a bottle of Monthélie to drink that night. I hadn't spent much time in Santa Cruz since the Bonny Doon days. Trevor talked nonstop about how epic Leslie was, a feeling that was allegedly mutual. This was an amusing, recurring theme with Trevor, and the mutuality part was almost always news to each girl in question. It was already Saturday afternoon, a beautiful one at that, but with each passing hour of daylight came the realization that I had some decisions to make about where I was going to be living and working for the rest of the year. While walking in the late day sunshine, I called my mentor Tasha at Whitethorn Winery and left a message asking for her professional advice about something.

The night turned into a drunken haze. Back in Petaluma and many bottles of wine later, I serenaded the girl Trevor was in love with, who clearly wasn't interested in him. As she got up to use the bathroom, I reached for the bottle of Monthélie and a corkscrew. "Don't crack that for Leslie, bro," Trevor advised me. "My palate is cooked and she'll drink anything."

"I'm gonna open it." She reemerged and got a grouchy glare from Trevor as he passed her on his way to his room alone. I poured up two glasses and picked up my guitar again.

It was a rocky, wasted performance on my part. We hadn't eaten enough at Trevor's friends' place earlier in the evening. I played Kris Kristofferson, tried Sufjan Stevens (but forgot some verses), "Lookin' for a Lover" by Neil Young, then a song of my own. We were on opposite couches and had both remarked on Trevor's moodiness that night. She had a wise, sarcastic sense of humor, a bit of an East Coast accent, and was definitely attractive in her own way. Spinning from all the wine from the day, we put on the TV and I adjusted the supermarket-bright lighting and joined her on the couch. We sipped the Burgundy swiftly as she clicked around to try to find "The Daily Show," claiming Jon Stewart was the sexiest man alive. She couldn't find the channel but said she could pull some clips up online. We headed into the office nook; she sat in Trevor's desk chair and I crouched beside her. The room was dark. My arm was around the top of her chair, then three minutes in I let it fall to the back of her bare neck and went right into a well-received massage. That lasted for about five minutes. She shut his computer off when the clip was done, and we went back into the living room. This time she sat on my left. It must've been past one in the morning by then. I kept rubbing her neck and she was closing her eyes and flexing her shoulders into it, then, when I finally thought it was appropriate, I started pulling her in for a kiss. She suddenly widened her eyes and turned her cheek.

"Whoa, wait. Trevor would *really* hate us after we did that," she said.

"He hates us already, anyway."

"No, I'm... I'm a sucker for a neck massage." She covered her eyes with her palms. "God, I gotta remember how forward guys are out here compared to home."

"Really?"

"Yeah, they've got no game."

"Oh, I feel bad for tryin'."

"No don't. I shouldn't have... Look, I'm really selfish. If I see a neck massage opportunity, I take it."

"Right."

"And I, I've got this boyfriend and he's in New York, and I really need to do something about it."

"How often do you see him?"

"He flies out one weekend, I'll go another one. We went to Greece in the spring."

"That's a lotta work."

"And that's the thing that got us into a big fight the other night is 'cause Trevor wants to be in a relationship with me and I can't."

"Really? See, he never puts it that way to me."

"Oh yeah? I was trying to, you know, be good and set boundaries, but he wanted to be more."

"Oh, so he *is* gonna hate both of us," I said. She nodded in the dim blue light of the living room. I let my arm drape up and around her on the couch, but the massage was done.

After talking some more, she stood up.

"Come back down soon," she said before stepping outside, leaving the smell of her freshly lit cigarette inside the familiar living room.

CHAPTER 11

With no call back from my mentor Tasha from Whitethorn Winery, whose feedback on my "should I stay or should I go" situation at Hirsch would've counted the most, I drove north on Sunday with the decision that I would be packing up and moving. My friends Mourad and Greta in Arcata had offered me a room to sleep in that night, breaking up my trip to Oregon. I hadn't committed to Rob officially, but he said he'd take me if I showed up. I was buzzing with anxiety. I got gas at a Chevron in Santa Rosa, then finally picked up the cell phone as I got on the freeway and called David Hirsch. I was surprised that he answered on the second ring.

"This is David."

"David, it's Darren."

"Who?"

"Darren," I repeated. He still wasn't getting it, so I tweaked a little New York City accent into it. "Darr-en!" I said.

"Oh! Darr-en! How are ya? Say, we looked for you yesterday to see if you were goin' to Barbara's party. You know, the Coyote Picnic."

"Oh no, I—"

"Yeah, Marie and I checked the trailer. I saw you drive out on Friday."

I paused before going into it. "Hey David, I've gotta talk to you about something. I-I don't think things—it's not working out, and I need to talk to you about that."

"What happened?"

"I… I don't think it's a healthy work environment."

"What?"

"Not with the vineyard or the trailer or anything, I just don't feel compatible with Mick. Comfortable is the word, not compatible."

"Would you mind going into more detail than that?"

"He's very difficult to work for. And I gave it, you know, gave it a while, knowing it was a big stressful week with the racking and all. But he's too, I don't know, he's not patient at all and has me walking around working all nervous and worried. I'm worried that I'm gonna mess something up all the time."

"Oh, okay, okay. So it's a personalities conflict that's going on. Look, Darren, when Mick is—how can I say this?—under pressure, he's got a very serious way, an intense way, of reacting. You've gotta not put yourself out there personally. It's not you, you know what I'm saying? That's how he works."

"But he really snaps on both me and Barbara. And if you have to ask him the same question twice, watch out. But it's carrying over into the trailer after work."

"Oh, oh I see." Now I got his attention.

"Thursday, toward the end of work, I felt like I irritated him so much that I just took my dinner and went into my little room and ate my dinner on the airbed. Just to get out of his way."

"Well, this can't be happenin'. Look here, Darren, I urge you to hang in there, and, and I'll talk to Mick and it won't be like, 'Hey Mick, Darren says' or anything like that. But this has to be addressed. You guys—to work—you guys have to be comfortable around each other for this to happen. So Darren, tell you what—we consumed too much wine at the party last night and I'm working on the copy for the new label and trying to get my mind wrapped around this. Where are you now?"

"I'm just getting onto River Road off 101."

"Well let's talk today or, let me see. Tell you what, Mick isn't coming out tomorrow I don't think, but let's you and I sit down and talk about this. If not tonight, then tomorrow. We'll talk it over, then I'll talk to Mick, and then you and Mick can talk it over. I don't know. But…"

"And David, I really like you and love this place, and I proved that I'll work hard and long here, I'm just afraid I'll be too nervous to learn anything."

"All right Darren. Say, I really appreciate you talking to me about this. Really. Thank you. So come on out, and tomorrow we'll have a conversation about it. We'll talk it over."

As I hung up, a nervous sensation coated my stomach. This was going to be the most awkward work experience of my life. I swiftly gobbled a stomach pill. I'd been taking one a day in light of all of this pressure. Mick would certainly boil over, his skin turning an even brighter red, and either hate me publicly or hate me passive aggressively. Or both. It wasn't like he was going to physically attack me on sight, but I doubted any loving bond could grow out of such soil. Maybe I'd suffer a weird behavioral pattern as a side effect from being made to feel irritating and incompetent every day of the week. All I knew was that as soon as either the name-calling started up or I contracted athlete's foot from him, I was good and gone.

I circled back into Santa Rosa after the call, wondering what to do with myself on a Sunday afternoon that I'd originally planned on using for the jailbreak. Heading to Healdsburg, I sat in a wine bar and caught up on email with a glass of Navarro Gewürztraminer. The girl behind the bar had a nice mix of music playing, which inspired me to take my acoustic demo CD up to her and mention that I was interested in performing there sometime if they liked what they heard. "Oh, thanks," she said blankly. I'm sure it made it right in with that evening's recycling.

* * *

Later on, with provisions in tow, I made it back up Bohan Dillon Road to the trailer, still disbelieving the fact that I was staying. I'd already removed myself from this place. It *was* comforting to know I'd have the trailer to myself for the night. Once inside, I reverted to my married–time tactics of when my ex and I would go stay with her mother in Shell Beach. Fights between the two strong-minded women surely erupted at least once during a weekend stay. After one too many nervous, drawn out occasions of having to pack up and ditch the spoiled scene after such a faceoff, I started setting up our luggage like little shelves and eating every dinner at her house with my shoes on and the car keys safely in my pocket. I made sure my closet at Hirsch was simplified into the luggage and two boxes, ready to go in two trips out the door. I wished there was some magical wand David could wave over Mick's head to exorcise the demon that was darkening his soul at work.

After prepping for another jailbreak, I turned on some music and whipped up a Pacific Northwest *charcuterie* plate of smoked salmon and three cheeses. I decided to open something stellar, so it was the Melville Carrie's Pinot Noir, with a thick red wax dip at the top that I melted off with my lighter. Full raspberry jam and vanilla and rocks flavored the nose of the Melville, which was a dark bomb of a wine at 15.8 percent alcohol.

I called Trevor from the back deck with a Riedel Pinot glass full of it. I guess he *did* enjoy hanging out with me more than he'd let on in the morning. He was surprised to hear that I was still at Hirsch.

"I thought you'd be on the highway to Humboldt with your life packed into your truck," he said. I explained my half-packed theory and how anything could happen this week.

"Gnarly," he said. "So David is investing quite a bit into you. I knew that was going to happen."

"How?" It was quiet as usual outside. The lazy afternoon sun sifted through the redwood trees above.

"At the Pinot Days tasting in the city, I went up to him and told him 'My friend Darren will be working for you,' and he said 'Oh yeah. We're really excited to be working with Darren. He's really great.'"

"Why didn't you tell me that this weekend?"

"I didn't want to further inflate the ego of someone that calls me delusional."

"Oh, don't take that seriously, like I don't take it seriously when you insult my good taste in music."

Deep down, he wanted to know if his love interest and I had hooked up the night before. I could've ended his inquisition by telling him the truth, but I left him guessing and ended the call. Since he was in another relationship, he deserved the suspense.

Soon the Carrie's was making me feel a little more at home on the hill. I played guitar for nearly two hours before drifting away on a tide of high alcohol Pinot and the comfort of knowing Mick wouldn't be there in the morning.

CHAPTER 12

Waking up on a workday without the sound of Mick's rubber sandals creeping down the hallway or his coffee grinder blaring was a godsend—but I could've used the noise since it was close to seven. I nearly went back to the Rooibos tea routine, but decided to nix that idea and grind up some Ethiopian coffee before I ate granola, then rushed across to the winery in the fog.

The winery door was locked, but the office was open. It was quiet. At the far end of the lab, Barbara was sitting at the table, looking over the grape cluster count sheets and vineyard maps. She was pretty tentative with me at first, so I assumed David spoke to her about my concern. She gave me the validated news that Mick wasn't coming in and that we'd be off by noon after going out to count grape clusters in two separate sections of the vineyard.

Counting grape clusters on the vine was a random process. It was a tactic to determine the yield in advance so the winery had enough tanks or bins to handle the incoming fruit (a problem they'd encountered in the harvest the previous year). Most of the arms of the vine trunks nearly grew right into each another, with shoots interloping at times. Some vines were holding 50 or more clusters apiece in blocks four and eleven, but a second thinning of fruit by the vineyard crew was coming on. The thinning entailed cutting off oddly formed or excessive clusters so the vine could put all of its energy into the healthiest of clusters. We also had to count clusters in famous block eight, which apparently was the source of some of the finest fruit grown on the property. Barbara and I recorded all of our counts on pads of paper. It was the perfect type of Monday for me to ease back in and just the type of work scene I had signed up for.

When we got to block eight, David was up on the steep Chardonnay hill thinning clusters with his crew. The reclusive vineyard manager Everardo Robledo and his family had just returned from vacation, and he was up on the hill running things. Barbara and I grabbed our clipboards and headed toward the opened gate.

"Hold on a second, Barbara," David said, coming down the slope. He looked at me. "Good Morning, Darren. Great to see ya." He had his usual blue button-up on, but it looked like it'd been washed over the weekend. He asked us where we counted already and then showed us some of the Chardonnay clusters on the ground that they'd just thinned, glowing fluorescent green in the sunlight.

"That must make ya crazy," Barbara said to him.

"Not anymore. I just had to realize that it's the job."

"And you said it'll make a better product?"

"Yeah, I think the Chardonnay's gonna be great this year – all these concentrated berries."

I touched one of the surviving clusters, miniature enough to fit two in my hand. They were cartoonish and compact.

We headed to the backside of the vineyard block and parted ways to count clusters on one of the Pinot blocks. Depending on how many vines were in the row, we'd count the clusters on every fourth or eighth vine and come up with an average for that section of the vineyard.

"We're gonna go back and get these figures done," Barbara called out to David on our way to her truck. The crew of a dozen guys was sweating up on the slope in the late morning heat. It was so steep that if your footing went out, you'd easily tumble down the hillside. One of the guys had sprained an ankle this season already.

David asked us about the empty barrels outside and mentioned that we needed to get them Borax'd. Wood-boring beetles eat holes right out of the barrels causing leaks and have an affinity for certain pricey forests of wood, such as Allier and Vosges.

"The older empties really need to get washed and moved out of the sun," he mentioned.

"We need more of the Borax stuff," Barbara said. "I can see if I can get some when I head into town later."

"Well, wait till we get more of that to treat them with first." Then David turned to me and said, "Listen Darren, why don't you come on down to the house to talk and have some stew."

"All right. What time's good?"

"Give me an hour," he said. I was excited as I followed Barbara back to her truck. I'd never been inside his place before, with its views of a bluff to the northwest. Barbara told me it was the original sheep rancher's house and that David had really fixed it up over the years.

We went back to the winery, filled out our cluster count averages, and then called it an early one. At the trailer, I chilled a glass-top Pinot Gris from Solena in Oregon and showered. I got lost on the way down to David's, missing an abrupt right hand turn and ending up where we'd done the cluster counts. David called me on my cell as I turned around.

"Hey Darren, where are you at?"

"I'm a minute away," I said, charging back up the dirt road.

"Good, I'm gettin' hungry down here."

David's dusty truck was out front and it looked like Marie was off in town. I passed by a black cat and knocked on the sliding glass door.

"Come on in, Darren," he said, wearing reading glasses and seated at a desk. "Just working on the copy."

"Oh. Copy? Is that for the website?"

"Yeah. I keep getting sidetracked. And plus, it's…" he made a negative gesture, "writing."

"Not a fan?" I asked.

"Oh, I am. I love to write. I've been working on a book, but once again, it's one of many things."

"Wow." I almost told him about trying and failing to sell a novel over the last three years, but you really shouldn't bring up such depressing things to a guy who hasn't yet finished his first book. Guess that comes later.

The kitchen in his house was packed with stuff: bottles, oils, spices, vegetables, pots, and pans. Books spilled off a few shelves, with varying subjects such as Kierkegaard, Le Montrachet, Mario Batali, *Everything is Illuminated*, Burgundy, Yoga, and lots of literary criticism. The view through the windows behind the couch and kitchen table was stunning, with no sign of humanity. It was a pretty cozy scene with a nice wood stove at the center. It'd be fair to think that David would have a big estate house or something, but this joint was right out of the man's Santa Cruz mountain era. It was comforting to see.

David stood up and led me to the dining room table.

"Well go ahead and sit. Let me get this stew out. Picked up some bread from the farmer's market that'll go really well with it."

He put down two bowls of stew, with a huge knuckled bone plopped right in the middle of mine. It looked like a bat skull or something. He motioned at the bottle I was holding, so I handed it to him to open. He went for a corkscrew, then looked at the top of the bottle and said, "So is this a screwcap or what?"

"No, it's one of those glass tops."

"No kidding. Glass? How does that work?"

"I think we foil cut it, then it twists off." David did just that. When he twisted, the little glass top flew right off onto the table.

"That's great!" he exclaimed.

"I guess the winemaker says the glass top thing appeals to women."

"Oh definitely," he said, picking it up and examining it, holding it close to his mustache. He poured us glasses and grabbed us forks before sitting down at the head of the four-top table.

"So," he began, "Mick was very nonplussed when I called him about the whole thing. He was professional—he didn't get to a personal level—but he seemed wholly surprised. And I asked Barbara, I said 'Barbara, last week, did Mick seem out of the ordinary?' And she said it was more the opposite. That he was mellower than usual."

"Don't scare me," I said, laughing nervously.

"No, I know, but I talked to him this weekend to see if he was relaxing or anything, and his wife had him doing yard work and fixing things. So whenever you have a guy with a lot of stress or under a lot of pressure, you can count on most of it stemming from what's going on at home."

"Right."

"I didn't know you'd gotten burned on Friday."

"Yeah."

"Is it okay?"

My arm was near bubbling, with two massive red marks down it. "Yeah, Barbara gave me some stuff for it. Mick was so intense and irritated that I was afraid to tell him about it. Then when I told him, he said 'sorry,' but then got right back into the mode. He didn't say take a break or anything. In fact, he wanted me to finish pressure washing the floor, but Barbara told him it wasn't a safe idea, so he got irritated about that."

I thought describing the strange, post-work trailer scene would paint more of a picture of the whole thing.

"Well, Darren, this place, it attracts people who don't come for a social outlet," he delivered with a grin, then took a big sip of the Pinot Gris. He examined the bottle. "Now I know why these people in Oregon are so proud of this stuff." He set the bottle down on the table. "Darren, if you came out here to meet people and socialize, then you came to the wrong place." He talked about last year's intern named Chris who was a rock climber, the same guy Mick had told me about. Fresh out of UC Davis, he wanted to work in the vineyard and the winery and rock climb all over the estate. He never really left the trailer for the first month. Ultimately, right before the first vineyard block was harvested, he went down to the Bay Area to hang out with some friends on the Friday before Labor Day, and David gave him a few bottles of the estate Pinot to drink. The guy drove back up to the ranch and packed his things that Sunday, drove to a vineyard block where David was working and said, "You guys are too tense. It's too much. I came here for fun, but it's all work."

"And I said to him, 'Chris, it's not like making a bad batch of beer and being able to dump it out and go again. This is one shot here. It's all we got.' And he said 'It's not for me. Sorry.' And then he left."

Sitting there at the table, I was glad that I hadn't done the same thing, though I was certainly ready to for all the same reasons.

"Look," I explained, "I'm sure Mick is a nice guy. Just, with my stomach condition, I can't handle the stress of last week again."

"Stomach condition? What's that?"

"I have acid reflux and I've ended up in the hospital twice over it."

"Acid reflux?"

"Yeah. Like extreme heartburn, but with me it led to vomiting and things like that."

"No kidding."

"I've been taking a pill a day for it. But the pills apparently cause stomach cancer in lab rats, so I don't know what's worse."

I almost brought my diary along to better explain the hostilities of the week, since I wasn't saying anything about it that seemed nearly serious enough to David. I was looking pretty ridiculous actually. Then I brought up something minor in my opinion.

"But with Mick though, David, I'm sure he's a good guy outside of work. You know, I hear him up late at night talking baby talk to his dog Cornelius on the couch and I—"

David stopped everything and said, "All right! We're gettin' ya outta there, Darren." He smacked the tabletop with finality. That was all I had to say. The visual of his pissed off winemaker embracing his sled dog and whispering sweet, late-night nothings to him clarified the entire insane situation or something.

David eloquently quoted philosopher Thomas Mann about the matter and related it to our situation. Something about us not being that different from Joseph and the apostles, and Mick and the Mexicans in the converted barn even. With our bowls of stew all bread-wiped clean, he suggested a few plans of action.

"Marie had a great idea. Right away when I told her what was happening she said, 'We must separate them immediately.' So here."

He pushed up from the table and I followed him outside and up the steps toward the guest unit across the way. Boxes cluttered the front porch and a dead tree with a massive old wasp nest had been trained up through a hole in the little deck. We stepped inside and there was a kitchenette, an actual bed, a large bathroom and closet, a desk, some décor in the form of an Eric Clapton concert poster, and no mouse droppings to boot. I'm sure their cats enforced that.

"This looks cool," I said.

"So listen, the guys working on the cooling need to stay in here through Friday, so we'll move you in that evening. What do you think?"

"I love it. I'm happy with this."

"I'll get some of this crap out of here," he said, waving his hand at the stacked boxes around the refrigerator. "This is a new refrigerator too," he said, opening it up and closing it proudly. "You know, Darren, maybe we can help each other out. This weekend we've got this wine dinner in the city. Are you good with cats?"

"Yeah, pretty good." I did have an allergic past with the felines, but all David asked was if I'd feed them in the morning and let them in their house at night.

"We've let them fend for themselves before out here, but it lowers their life expectancy significantly."

"Sure, that'd be fine."

"Good. Marie'll be so pleased. Really."

We wandered back into his house. Sitting at the table, we finished our glasses of wine and talked about how to deal with the rest of the issue. He suggested the three of us having a chat, and then mentioned having Barbara in on it too.

"If you guys are going to do this thing, you've gotta be harmonious. Otherwise it won't work. And look, it's the harvest. Things break, people fuck up, it happens. But look, we're going to go big time here and have a roundtable discussion. I mean, are you okay with that?"

That sounded good for a second before souring in my mind. It'd just be too strange. "Or, you and Mick can have a one on one about it."

"You know, let me do that, David. I'll go for it."

"You're comfortable with that?"

"Yeah, I think I can do it."

He seemed impressed, then said, "You know, our motto for the harvest was going to be 'Getting the Vine Ripe.' Every year, everyone is so focused on getting the fruit ripe, but that's only one part of the vine's cycle. It carries through to dormancy, and pruning, and fertilizing. But here's the thing, I'm thinking now it should be more, something like 'Harmonizing with the Site and Each Other.'"

"I like it."

Things were getting really Northern Californian in here, and I felt like I was to blame for it. When did I become such a hippie?

"Alright. That's fantastic. Well, that's it." He stood up and I followed suit, walking out onto the front porch. That black cat was out there and David called to it. The name must've been Russian or Northern European because I didn't understand it. The cat rolled around playfully on the warm concrete.

"You know Darren, I'm impressed. A lot of people sweep their problems under the rug. You wasted no time with that. You just stared it down and brought it right into the light."

"With my stomach and all, I don't think I could go any other way anymore."

"It's important to me that you're comfortable here. I'm always amazed by anybody who'd want to drop everything and come to live and work out here. It's a rare thing."

* * *

A few hours later I called Rob to talk while I boiled potatoes. When I mentioned the changes and the confrontational situation on deck for tomorrow, he pointed out how it could go only two ways—good or bad—and most likely extreme variations on each. The bad could consist of Mick greeting me with a, "Darren, good morning, have some coffee and then clean the toilets." I could picture that too. With an intensely emotional day on the horizon, Rob urged me to "Get shit-faced drunk tonight, Darren. Pop somethin' killer and relax."

After dinner, I washed the dishes and became really nervous about the next day—but not as nervous as I would have been without a Plan B. The sun couldn't set any faster. I thought about Trevor's ego-throttled solution to the problem, which entailed grabbing my best bottle and sitting down with Mick in the trailer and going, "Bro, I know you've been going through some shit, but you've sort of been a dickhead all week. Let's drink some killer shit and get over it!" Trevor's boisterous persona made him the only person who could get away with that.

I was nearly through a delicious bottle of Pikes Shiraz. Full eucalyptus trees, sweet oak and chocolate aromatics, with a rich and resolved finish. The song "Best of All Possible Worlds" by Kristofferson played on my laptop, and I was about ready to watch a movie and crash. I'd be up and working in nine hours. I kept obsessing on how this would play out. I thought back on the conversation I had with my dad earlier in the afternoon. He was excited to hear from me, but always quick to get off the phone or be the first to terminate the conversation. I told him things were tense and not going as well as I expected. He was shocked to hear that the winemaker wasn't being very friendly to me.

"How could he not like a Delmore?" he said in his patented whine. "We're all about company!"

CHAPTER 13

I met Barbara in the office the next day, and we went in to check that the silicone bungs were still lodged into all the barrels in the cellar. Sometimes the wine inside can still be active and produce enough pressure to blast the bungs out of the barrels, allowing fruit flies or oxygen to taint the wine. Our conversation centered on her and her husband's belated trip into Yountville the day before to get their hunting tags for the upcoming deer season. It occurred to me that not only had this nice country woman blasted a good dozen deer in her lifetime, she'd also skinned, bled, and butchered them. No wonder working here amid such human hostility seemed tame to her.

I cursed the sun as it rose higher and higher and the hour got closer to Mick's arrival time of ten. My stomach was well under attack with the apprehension. I took my pill in the morning just in case. Barbara and I went out to count clusters in blocks 4A and 4B. The world kept on spinning, and soon it was time to head back to the lab to add up our figures and face the music.

I didn't see Mick's truck there yet, so we went inside and started tallying up our cluster counts and then divided them by the amount of samples done. As Barbara started copying off maps and block sheets for my clipboard, Mick came in with a new dust head for cleaning.

"Hey guys," he said in an oddly friendly tone.

"Hi Mick," Barbara said.

"Morning," I offered with my eyes to the papers before me.

"Look what I've got, Barbara," he said, proudly holding the dust mop like it was the gift she'd been dreaming of.

"Wow, how exciting" she said sarcastically.

Mick sat down at his desk and turned on his computer. Barbara took a seat at the table next to me as I organized all of the maps and the vine and block data sheets. The room grew silent. Mick asked Barbara about the pressure washer rifle that he was going to UPS back to the company for repair. It'd been boxed up in the back since Friday, ready to go.

"Okay, okay," he said, keeping it calm.

"Did ya bring Cornelius with you?" she asked.

"I did. He's at the trailer." He asked about the vineyard blocks that we went out to and what the counts were looking like before telling Barbara a few final things to do for the day and urging her to get going early. Then he looked at me and said, "Darren, go ahead and do a bung check in the new barrel room. I'm going to do some work on the computer, then you and I are going to head out for lunch to spend some time getting to know one another." He gave me an intense nod with a smile of sorts.

"Sounds good, Mick," I said, keeping my own tone as lively as possible.

"We'll head out about 12:30."

* * *

Mick pulled his truck up to the crush pad, and I got in the passenger side. I was wondering where we were going to lunch, since the closest place was 45 minutes away. I was nervous but rolling with it. Cornelius was in the back, his big mouth open with his tongue hanging out. Instead of taking Bohan Dillon Road, Mick crossed over the cattle guard and down the secret road that lead to Fort Ross School.

It was a touch eerie, heading down that dirt road into the heavy forest. It was an old logging road, not patrolled by any law enforcement agency, and as I was about to see, it dropped down a good 600 feet and then climbed back up 1000. He could have killed me and buried me out there and no one would've known for days.

"I don't know where Darren went," I could picture him telling Barbara and David in the afternoon. "Guess he quit like Chris did!"

Mick broke the silence. "So Darren, tell me about last week."

"Well, it was a big challenge, and, well, I got the impression that you hated my guts."

"Really? What gave you that idea?"

"I just felt that, that, I don't know. That I irritated you to such an extent that I felt useless. Worthless. You looked physically irritated by me on a number of occasions and were snapping."

"Really?" He frowned at that and kept his eyes on the switchbacks down the mountain. "Well," he started, "while last week was an extremely stressful situation for everybody, let me say I am sorry that you felt that way. Racking is the most sensitive time in the winery since we never filter, and it is a very stressful part of the process up here. It didn't help that you landed here just in time for it, but that's how things worked out, and we got through it. These next few weeks will be much more like it normally is up here. We'll be doing very little in the cellar, and you'll be out working in the vineyard and getting acquainted with the different vineyard blocks."

I didn't know what to say to that. We were deep down in the woods now, and we approached a wobbly-looking bridge that crossed over a creek without any railings.

"I may have been pushing you harder than Barbara or anyone else because I have a higher expectation of you, with your background at Tasha's and elsewhere. Barbara has made it clear that she is just here for the job. She has no interest in taking classes, going to tastings, or wine in general." There was a slight pause. "Did Tasha filter her wines?" he randomly asked.

"No, I don't think so. She had something in the line to the bottling tank I think, but no pads or diatomaceous earth or anything."

"Okay. Okay."

"I just wonder, I mean, if racking was that intense, then what's bottling or harvest gonna be like? You know?"

"Well, you'll have to ask yourself if winemaking is really what you want to do. And what kind of wines you want to make. With Syrah or Cabernet, you can be a cowboy. With Pinot Noir, the whole process, from the soil to bottle, is much more complicated. I know you've done a variety of things in the wine industry, but I don't think you've mentioned that winemaking is ideally what you're looking to do."

"I think it is."

We drove up alongside a couple living areas and then, on the right, the Fort Ross School. Mick slowed to a stop and opened up the new *Wine and Spirits Magazine* that had been resting on the console. He flipped to a page of wine reviews, and there was the Hirsch Estate Pinot Noir, garnering a 93 point score and a flattering review that mentioned Mick's name.

"That was my first full year up here, that's what we got, and that is where I intend to keep it. These are serious wines. Yes, we will have some... some fun.

But we are making serious wine, and a lot of the time we are intense about it." He paused and reached behind his seat, pulling out a bottle of wine. "I brought this for you too." He handed me the bottle: Pride Cabernet Franc.

"Cool," I said, checking out the label. "Thanks. My friend says this stuff is really good." The bottle was trembling in my hand.

He nodded with intensity and got out of the truck, corralling Cornelius into the kennel behind our seats, Cornelius didn't appreciate it all too much, but it was the new law. Mick hopped back in the truck and we headed down Seaview Road, with views of the sparkling blue ocean to our right.

"Last year, after Chris quit, we made six thousand cases of wine with myself, Barbara and a cocktail waitress from Fort Ross. And Barb wasn't driving a forklift yet. I have full faith that we will get through this, but you've gotta be able to commit."

I felt inspired then. I wanted to defy the notion that I was known to quit when the going got rough, the very thing my ex-wife had accused me of before. I knew it was a dangerous world I was choosing to reside in, full of hostility and mood swings, but I proclaimed it anyway.

"I am committed to working this harvest at Hirsch."

Mick nodded and extended his hand for a hearty shake. "Good. Good."

We drove along the ridge in silence, maneuvering through some curves bordered by thick parcels of forest.

"And I understand David is offering you the cabin, I think that's great. No hard feelings at all for that. If you need to microwave your lunch at the trailer or make coffee, by all means you're welcome to do that."

Mick pointed to our left at a black mailbox. "So that's Seaview Winery. We'll have to go taste there with their winemaker Neil before harvest. He was out tasting with us not too long ago."

"That'd be cool."

He pointed at another property that looked suspicious with its government style fencing and heavily posted "No Trespassing" signs. "And I think that is the gate to Peter Michael."

"That is the steepest vineyard I think I've seen," I said.

"They should be getting fruit for the first time from it this harvest."

It was a clean, still August day, and the ocean was glassy and endless. As we dropped down Meyers Grade Road, Mick said, "I asked my wife about this whole thing and she says I can be very difficult to work for. If I am being an ass, let me know. I have worked for a string of asses over the years, and I certainly don't want to become one."

"Okay." I laughed nervously.

There were cows on our right and left as we descended closer to sea level.

"Now these up here are some of Barbara's cows."

"No way." I'd heard how Barbara's husband managed some cattle and that she would help him out during the afternoon and on the weekends. "She was so excited about deer season opening this Saturday."

"That is completely an entirely different reality," Mick said.

"I know. I've never skinned an animal or anything."

"That woman has been up to her armpit in some cow's ass before," he said.

On Highway One, we pulled up to the only restaurant in Jenner called River's End. The place overlooked the mouth of the Russian River and seemed deserted. We got out of the truck and walked up to the door and pulled on it to no avail. In the span of the ride down, I'd formulated the fantasy of having some never-ending salmon luncheon, with Mick and I toasting each other over a magnum of Kistler Chardonnay on the Hirsch company card. With respect to reality, The River's End was closed Tuesdays and Wednesdays.

Back in the truck, we pulled up to the little riverside espresso place by the gas station. There was a hippie teenage girl working inside.

"Do you have sandwiches?" Mick asked when we walked in.

"Yeah, we have some."

He pulled out his credit card and the girl said, "Oh, we only take cash or checks."

"Really?" Mick was not excited about that. In fact, his skin was beginning to take on that familiar red flush.

He quietly devised a backup plan and we headed in on 116 toward Guerneville, stopping in the little town of Duncans Mills. We parked by the general store where some tourists were milling around. We ordered sandwiches from two rural women working the place, who quickly let us know that they were *out of a lotta stuff.*

After ordering, Mick led the way and grabbed a 22-ounce Lagunitas IPA from the fridge. I took a look at the beers and settled on a Butte Creek organic porter. I sat on a little bench to wait while Mick roamed around the dusty, poorly stocked space, probably wondering if he was in complete hell having to do this. It seemed like he really didn't want to be there. The long silences and creased up frown lines were dead giveaways. Once our sandwiches were ready, I thanked Mick for lunch as we went outside and sat at a tiny, wobbly, wooden table. The women gave us Styrofoam cups for our beers. Mick stood and used his key ring opener to crack his first, then gave the opener to me. As he went to sit down, his knee came up and bumped the table, knocking over his beer. "Fuck!" he snapped in earshot of an elderly couple at one of the tables. They flashed him an offended look. I picked the bottle up and saved most of his foamy IPA.

* * *

On the drive back from lunch, we took Bohan Dillon Road and Mick pointed out each famous vineyard on the drive up. "So there's Peter Michael from this angle. There's Seaview. This is the start of Martinelli's property. Here's Marcassin's Blue Slide Ridge vineyard." It was a series of reminders about how much clout this whole area had going for it. He mentioned how he and his wife would like to find some plantable acreage and how they had been spending their weekends looking for it as far north as Potter Valley in Mendocino.

* * *

That night, Mick and I got drunk together. We were actually partying in the trailer with Cornelius if you can believe it. It was a relief to relax around each other with the great social lubricant of the vine. We went through quite a few bottles, from a "Pinkie" rosé from Fiddlehead Cellars, to Hirsch Chardonnay out of a plastic lab bottle, to a corked Pride Cabernet Franc, and finally a spontaneous Whitethorn Anderson Valley Pinot.

"The last Hirsch from Tasha had like seventeen percent alcohol!" Mick exclaimed.

I found out that Mick had nearly had it after last year's harvest here, all on account of too much stress. Mick also talked about the intern in 2004 that had an Asian girlfriend *and* an Asian mistress, and the fateful morning that he stayed in bed with his mistress instead of showing up for work. That was the morning that Mick fell on a one-ton bin while doing a punch-down and broke his collarbone and needed staples in his head. When he went down, the only person on the crush pad was a husky, shorts-wearing winemaker named George who was renting cellar space from David and making his own hand-destemmed Pinot Noir. George heard Mick yelling for help, and when George got to him, Mick's instructions were to get help, but not send a helicopter. The firemen from Fort Ross were miraculously there in eight minutes time, though the ambulance took an hour and a half. When Mick returned to work days later, he went into the trailer at nine a.m. looking for the intern as he was just getting up. The guy yawned and said to Mick, "You know what's horrible? I'm out of Lucky Charms."

"You're also out of a job," Mick informed him.

I was getting the feeling that this was an insane operation to work for. Maybe it was a matter of perspective. Grand Cru clout versus physical injury? Long hours, low pay, and a legacy of interns who couldn't make it versus a feather in my cap? The challenge was on.

We were up past midnight. Every bottle went down the hatch, even the corked Pride. Mick made some spicy polenta cakes that should've had me puking all those acids up, but, miraculously, didn't. We connected on a variety of topics, mostly wine related, but on a major canine note too. I mentioned the time when my ex-wife and I lived in Eureka and our two dogs were poisoned with antifreeze-coated rice that some evil dog killer chucked over the backyard fence. He sat right up on the futon looking physically repulsed by that story. Apparently he experienced the same thing first hand in Calistoga. He was adamant about how "fucked" that was and looked ready to roll out and kill.

CHAPTER 14

Two days later, Marie Hirsch called me up at the office to find out when she could talk to me about watching the cats that weekend. I said I'd be down to the house in ten minutes or so. Moments after hanging up, the office door flung open and in walked a formally dressed David Hirsch.

"Darren, call my wife!" he said.

"She just called me. I'll be down there in a few."

"Good. She'll be able to sleep tonight after you get that all squared away."

"Hey, you look good," I said.

"Yeah? Meeting with the bankers today, so…you know." He laughed and set down a bottle of wine with a horrible homemade label on it. "I want you and Mick to sit down and taste this. Now, it's homemade, but I want you to pay attention to the fruit."

I took the bottle and had a closer look at the label. It was a Cabernet Sauvignon in a Burgundy-shaped bottle. Hirsch Vineyard Cab on the horizon? The great tinkerer was at it again.

"Okay Darren, I'll see ya!" And he was out.

I drove down to the Hirsch residence—my future residence as well—and parked behind David's truck. He must've taken Marie's new BMW wagon to the meeting. I knocked lightly on the sliding glass door and patchouli-scented Marie appeared with her short, black, *Pulp Fiction*-style hair, the shade of which matched her top and shorts.

"How's it going, Marie?"

"Good Darren, good." In her Czech accent, she started to talk about the weather, their itinerary for the weekend, and then got right into mentioning some of my cat-sitting duties. She stopped and asked me, "Have you met them?"

"No, no, I uh, I haven't *met* them." I stopped and wondered what the hell we were talking about. Was I watching children or felines? "I saw a couple of 'em."

She went into the exotic names and three character traits of the cats — a shy one, a princess, and a lazy oaf. She showed me the airtight food container, the water bowl, and how to leave one door slightly open for the bashful one named Squeaks at night. The black cat Bobés had been bitten twice by a rattlesnake; a thousand bucks later, he was keeping on. Then Marie showed me the "movie room" with VHS tapes and DVD's lining the wall, but what snagged my attention was a huge collection of vinyl. She showed me the remote controls and told me to make myself at home while they were gone.

"You can cook something, use the stove, whatever is cool."

I spied the VHS box for *Ghost Dog: The Way of the Samurai*, which was one of my favorite indie movies of all time.

"No way! You have *Ghost Dog*?"

"Ah, yes. This is David's movie."

"I love that movie. I have the soundtrack too."

"He does too. He must've watched it like fifteen times already."

On the way out, she picked up two of the cats so I was able to pet a couple of them. Then she asked me, "How did it go with Mick?"

"You know, it went pretty good. We had lunch and talked about it. I think me living over here will be just as nice for him as it will be for me. Our own space. But we got drunk together the other night and connected a bit."

"Oh, good."

"You know what's funny, though, is that his dog was really skittish to me all last week and stuff, and after we got back from our lunch and talk—well that night—his dog jumped onto my lap and started rolling around and cuddled with me. He warmed up to me the same day."

"Right. Right. Animals, they can sense our energy."

* * *

After work that day, I was talking on the phone with the receptionist at my doctor's office with a glass of Sauvignon Blanc. There was this horrible clicking on the connection, even on the back porch, so I stepped away from the trailer in shorts and my sandals and walked down the steps beneath the redwood tree toward the clearing, asking all the while "Can you hear me? Can you hear me now?" As the cell reception got clearer in one spot, I paused and my eyes sifted through the grass and dried brown leaves around me, lighting on what at first looked to be a tree limb between my feet. The limb suddenly became shiny and fat and developed a particular pattern. I darted backwards just as I saw the full scale of what was laying between my bare feet. A snake, a huge snake. The longest snake I've ever seen, with plump girth to boot. As I stepped up to the safety of the steps to get a better overhead view, it slithered slowly on the downhill slope, then raised its tail in the air and I saw it. I saw its rattling jewelry raised high in the sky. And then I heard it. Like a percussionist for Carlos Santana, the thing filled the air with its defensive chatter, sending slivers of ice right through me. Even from 15 feet away and with easy access to the indoors, I felt like the rattlesnake could strike me. All the while the receptionist was hearing me drop numerous F-bombs and freaking out.

"I'm sorry, but there's like a massive rattlesnake in front of me, and I was just standing on top of it. It's the biggest snake I've ever seen!"

If I remembered correctly, this receptionist was attractive, but she had the most monotone way about her, which was even carrying over to what I was considering to be my near death via venom. "Whoa," she said without an ounce of feeling.

"I've never seen one in person, and I was standing right over the thing in sandals!"

"Oh, be careful." She got back to the nature of the call. "So, when is the best time for the doctor to reach you with your results from the upper endoscopy and stomach emptying examination?" It seemed like a different lifetime when I was in the radiology suite being analyzed, let alone with a camera down my throat. I would finally know whether or not something serious was going on inside of me, which seemed like a low priority compared to the imminent serpent in the leaves.

"Uh, a good time to reach me is from three on," I managed to commit to her, feeling electric.

"All right, I'll let the doctor know."

I charged back into the house and got my disposable camera to document the snake. Going back outside, it was still there, but further along on its retreat down the slope. I saw its tongue slithering. I damned myself for not having a legitimate camera with a zoom on it, but I snapped a pic anyhow.

It was only four p.m. and I was staying in for the night.

I physically shivered just thinking about walking the vineyard blocks and counting clusters. I must have been walking by dozens of rattlesnakes. The thought of that made me clench up and lift my feet off the ground as I sat in the kitchen.

I called Mick to warn him, since Cornelius usually ran around the back of the trailer before coming inside. With things going seemingly well between the two of us, a snakebite on his pride and joy was the last thing we needed going into bottling week.

CHAPTER 15

After cutting off clusters and bringing them back to the lab to weigh them for Mick's tonnage projections, my only job for the rest of Friday was to drive David to the Fort Ross School via the secret road and move out of the trailer. I picked him up at his place and we started bouncing along our way. We talked about the road, what it was like in the winter, and the winemaker dinner he was attending. I had a Townes Van Zandt CD playing that made him trail off mid-sentence and then ask who it was.

Marie's BMW was parked at Fort Ross School where she was waiting for him, so I pulled up alongside it and waved to her. David got out and started loading his luggage into her car. She gave me some finalized cat sitting instructions and plant watering requests, then they drove out ahead of me. With the whole day free, I drove down Seaview Road en route to Sebastopol, with a very vague shopping list and some emails to check at a faster pace than what was available at the ranch.

Trevor had talked about bringing Grace up to the vineyard to camp for the night, but with him being broke and without a job, I couldn't picture that happening. As I got into cell phone range, my phone beeped with lots of voicemails, and, upon checking them, discovered that they were in fact coming up for the whole weekend. Trevor was bringing a bunch of wine and she was going to bring her vaporizer, which meant it was up to me to make dinner. I called Trevor and told him I'd email directions and reminded him to make it before sundown, since I wouldn't advise anyone to tackle a darkened Bohan Dillon Road, let alone Meyers Grade. I also mentioned my rattlesnake run-in and questioned their outdoor intentions, to which Trevor said "Bro, my dad and I used to hunt those things when I was seven." So after getting a cappuccino at Roasters next to a laundromat on the south end of Sebastopol with my laptop going, I picked up a Copper River Sockeye salmon from the Safeway in Guerneville and returned to the ranch to move and make some herbs de Provence seasoned salmon and caramelized onion mashed potatoes in my new abode. There was something divine about cooking in the country. With such isolation and no need to drive anywhere, drinking wine, blasting music, and cooking for hours seemed to be about as good as it gets in the hills.

I was on glass number two or three when they got to the winery around ten o'clock. I drove up to meet them under a sky alive with stars. Once I got close, I saw a truck parked with its lights off. Trevor flashed them on and off when I came into range, so I flipped a U-turn and led them down to the new residence.

Trevor introduced me to Grace when they got out of the truck. She was small and busty, with a wide smile, pale skin, and dark, short hair. She was wearing old jeans and a pinkish-orange tie-dye t-shirt. Sure enough, she'd brought her boxy, brown vaporizer and plugged it into the wall in my new cottage before their bags were brought in. After some accelerated smoking and tasting of the bottles Trevor brought with him, we dined on the floor around my little round table, joking that this was the best restaurant in town. I talked about the rattlesnake situation and the alleged population of mountain lions and bears around the ranch. Grace listened for the most part, drank at the same pace as Trevor and I, and blazed heavily. Before we knew it, it was well after midnight and they were setting up in the back of his truck (as per my elevated camping recommendation). Before following Grace out into the night, Trevor paused.

"I'm scared, bro," he said with a hand on my shoulder. He had thrown on a black hooded San Francisco Giants sweatshirt.

"I know," I said with a nod and zero consolation, washing the dishes all stained with Barbara's blackberry pie that we had devoured. I wasn't going out there.

As the crickets and frogs raged on in a thunderous, nocturnal chorus around Trevor and Grace, camo-fashioned hunters were also drinking coffee and driving their 4X4's all over the property with rifles and binoculars on the first night of open deer season. Barbara and her husband were among them with two tags apiece. Trevor and Grace ultimately stripped down in the back of his truck, tossed their underthings to the dirt, and fucked beneath a meteor shower.

* * *

The next morning, I fed the cats and let them loose into the morning sun. I tried talking to them as Marie had encouraged me to do, trying out lines like "Good morning Bobés, how'd you sleep?" and "Hey Minka, you look nice this morning," and "Here comes Squeaks!" Afterward, I passed by Trevor's truck and saw panties on the ground. Trevor stuck his head up out of a sleeping bag.

"We fully saw a mountain lion. Right up around that tree. It was heavy."

I toasted croissants and brewed up the East Timor coffee that Trevor brought up from his friend. We smoked, sipped and ate in the cottage.

"Last night was the best sex I've ever had," Trevor shared right in front of Grace. "Hands down. Under a meteor shower. Epic!" Grace grinned wide at that, smoking out of the vaporizer.

Amped off three French presses full of dark roast, we formulated a road trip to get some of the south swell I'd seen on a wave forecast online. We piled in my truck and began our journey down the secret road. Once down on Highway One, we sadly saw some white caps on the water already, so we drove north and landed in the town of Mendocino for lunch.

Trevor had told me he and Grace were covering lunch, but after sandwiches and local white wine, his credit card came back declined. He handled it well enough, but he was leaning his head upon his palm and tripping out a little at the table. Grace and I covered him and split the check.

We continued on to Fort Bragg, where Trevor and I had absolutely scored a beachbreak during a south swell the year before. Loaded with anticipation, we parked off the side of the highway and walked out on the ledge to see if we'd strike gold again. The beach looked nothing like its former beautiful self. It just looked like an empty, windblown beachbreak. The whole North Coast was out of the question as far as surfing for the day was concerned.

We headed back toward the vineyard and Grace paid for groceries at the Surf Supermarket in Gualala. Trevor announced that he'd make some chicken burritos and cook and clean it all up. I'd do the wines. Trevor ended up making good on his laborious contribution, doubling up the tortillas, seasoning the chicken, and making an amazing tray of food. I opened a Drew Weir Vineyard Pinot and a 1999 Whitethorn Cabernet.

"You don't have to open those, bro," Trevor said with widened eyes when I placed the bottles on the table.

"I know. It's cool."

* * *

Sunday morning opened up with Grace telling us about having sex in the shower with four other people. She certainly had a captive audience. During moments when she was in the bathroom or elsewhere, Trevor had bragged about how much of a freak she was. Over more coffee, as we talked about our upbringings, she shared how at her house her parents always had an opened copy of *The Joy of Sex* in the living room when she was really young. I shared how I'd never witnessed my parents kiss while they were together and that my dad yelled at me once for accidentally seeing him naked as he got out of the shower. Grace reminded me of my ex, talking so candidly about sex, group sex, girl-on-girl sex, everything. It was like one-upmanship almost, because in my ex's case it was more talk than action. I was getting the drift that Grace would probably have gotten down with both of us at the same time if Trevor had suggested it, since extraordinary experiences seemed to be part of her world.

We decided to go wine tasting, so we drove in on River Road and went to Joseph Swan winery. Afterward, we cut in to Woodenhead winery, a newer label that opened a tasting room in western Santa Rosa. Their Pinots tasted like Zins to me, and their Zins smelled like nail polish remover, which is the flaw of volatile acidity. Grace bought some wine, then we cut over to infamous Rochioli and tried a Sauvignon Blanc and one Pinot.

We were crammed into Trevor's front seat of his truck on the way back to the coast, and Grace started talking about sex again. Trevor was getting agitated about it, since he was now technically her boyfriend. She even mentioned how she wouldn't turn down a three way as we headed out of Guerneville along the river, before launching into how museums turn her on. I immediately said "There's the uh Fort Ross museum. Why don't we pull off before we head up the hill?"

* * *

On Monday, I made a dark brew out of the remaining East Timor grounds as the sun rose behind the cottage. I poured off a big cup, then politely got a thermos of it sealed up for the lustful campers outside. Trevor either truly loved it out here enough to stay the third night, or else was hell-bent on avoiding having to spend money on a campsite with insufficient funds. No biggie. Grace worked her designer magic and Feng Shui'd my room, provided erotic stories, good food, and nearly a hand job. It was nice to have them here on my first fully committed weekend in the cottage.

The day at work was mellow. I pressure-washed a portion of the barrel room with the repaired rifle. It was like hopping into the driver's seat after you'd been in a car accident. I also blasted eight new, small, open-top fermentation tanks with the hot, powerful stream, as well as the grape sorting trays. I relearned how to fill a propane tank. At lunch, I relaxed after some soup and a sandwich. I could sense that Grace had left a sexual aura in my little place.

After work I got the scheduled call from the ever-unenthused Rachel at Dr. Fulbeck's office. "You're borderline normal in regards to your rate of digestion," she said, "which is probably giving you acid reflux and heartburn. Possibly a little lazy stomach. So keep taking your Protonix pills and try to break up your meals to five smaller meals throughout the day."

Glad that $5,000 gave me such sensational medical advice.

"So regarding the endoscopy, did he see anything in there of concern?" I pressed her. He didn't, which was a dream come true. I thought I'd have scarring of tissue or an ulcer. But alas, there was nothing seriously wrong with me.

I was still sketched out to take walks around the property, so I embarked on a routine of 50 sit-ups and 20 push-ups. I hadn't surfed since that first weekend in Santa Cruz. Work had become fairly non-physical and peaceful, with Barbara and I wrapping the rest of the new tanks with insulating foam and doing some light cluster sampling out in the vineyard. The pace was sure to quicken the following week when we started bottling.

CHAPTER 16

On Tuesday of that week, David had a two-hour sit down with Mick. I think it was the "My Demands" meeting that David had mentioned when I had lunch with him beforehand. Needless to say, it made Mick look edgy and act like he'd pissed a hornet through his urethra. Luckily, my job assignments kept me away until 2:30 p.m. when Barbara and I had to weigh all the clusters we picked from various blocks, then tediously crush them in a colander to give the juice to Mick, who would run sugar, acidity, and PH tests. Barbara told me to add up all the cluster weights prior to crushing them, cancel out the heaviest and the lightest, then divide the total weight by the amount of samples to get our average gram weight per cluster. I put the finished sheets away in their respective parts of a three ring binder and closed it. I turned to start helping Barbara crush when Mick looked at me.

"What were the average weights?" he asked.

Damn. The sheets were all in different parts of the folder now, and I couldn't recall all the blocks we did.

I asked Mick "Which blocks?" He barked them off, one by one, so I rushed around that binder as quickly as I could and mixed one up with another. Though clearly irritated, Mick took a little time with me and, in the words of Barbara and that redneck comedian before her, "We got 'er done." She left at 3:30, yet Mick didn't tell me I could go. I went to check the bungs in the cellar and randomly tidy things up.

I came back into the office and Mick was still running the lab analysis on the juice samples. It was an important part of winemaking that I'd told him I wanted to learn while working here. He wasn't offering any instruction on this afternoon, so I didn't ask.

"Are you going to the Family Winemakers tasting on Sunday?" I asked after a couple minutes. His wife was on the board of directors and they were holding their big two-day tasting at Fort Mason in San Francisco on Sunday and Monday.

"Nope. I'll be here!" He didn't sound thrilled. Pronged in the ass maybe, but nothing like the guy who claimed, "I'm one of the few winemakers who actually enjoys bottling." I was already weary of the forthcoming bottling week. I had to remind myself not to take anything personally and to just try my hardest, work my smartest, and ask him for direction.

It was joyous to drive away from work now, instead of walking across to the trailer. Having my own space was working wonders. I played guitar for an hour at sunset, perched in the back of my truck, the sounds drifting off the silent ridge and heard by no one.

* * *

I was drinking a Talley Pinot Noir the next afternoon and putting the finishing touches on some egg flower soup when I heard David pull up on his quad runner. Marie, who was off in Fort Ross teaching yoga, had reiterated to him how my front door handle fell off and didn't work. It was now a handle-less hole with only the closing latch inside, turned by either a set of grape clippers or my new method of delicately sticking a chopstick through the nut and rotating it open.

"Hey Darren!" David said as he approached the front door.

"Hold on!" I replied. "I'm locked in here." I grabbed the token chopstick and maneuvered it through the nut, so from David's point of view he saw this chopstick coming out of the door. I failed three times to spin it open while he waited on the other side. I finally got it, turned it over, and opened the door.

I was playing a Lee Morgan CD on my laptop, and David worked on the handle while I finished grilling an accompanying sandwich. He eyeballed my bottle of Talley, but it was still early afternoon and I didn't think he wanted any.

"You really yanked on this thing," he said, revealing the sagging handle that he'd put back on. "Be really gentle with this. I'll try to fix it up a bit more."

"Thanks David," I said, watching his receding form move quickly out of sight.

CHAPTER 17

I took off around four on Friday for a trip into Sebastopol to see my favorite Argentinean, Nicolas. Heading into town entailed corralling any bills to mail out, bringing a cooler with blue ice in it to haul perishables back up, and packing my laptop for some Wi-Fi. Nicolas had worked with me at Eberle Winery in Paso Robles after he'd finished his studies at Cal Poly. Now he worked for a winery in Green Valley, and he and his wife Amber lived in a condo in Santa Rosa they bought at the height of the housing boom after returning from a stint in Mendoza, Argentina.

On the way out, I stopped by the winery and met the trucker Jake from the mobile bottling company. Mick had left earlier in the day, but had asked if I could show Jake around once he navigated the semi-truck up to the crush pad. I had no idea how he got a truck that size up Bohan Dillon Road, but he did. Jake was about my age and had just finished bottling up at Drew Family Winery in Anderson Valley.

"That guy makes good wines, man," I said to Jake.

"Oh, I know. I got to drink some of 'em. Cool property up there." I showed him our tanks and tried to answer his questions the best I could about the next week's shenanigans.

An hour later, I got into Sebastopol and confirmed with Nicolas that I was on my way to the Ace Cider House as planned. There were cars lined up around the industrial looking building on the corner of 116 and Graton Road. I circled around and then decided on the parking lot across the street. There was an outdoor BBQ scene consisting of hippies, rastas, punkers, cowboys, lesbian moms, farmers, hipsters and rednecks. An older guy in an apron barbecued oysters while live reggae was performed on the stage inside. I walked past people on the picnic benches outdoors and heard, "Hey Darren!" I looked to my left and saw, sitting across from a girl at a nearby table, Nicolas, a big smile stretched across his face. He stood and I gave him a hug.

"I like the beard!" he exclaimed.

"Saves sunblock."

"This is my friend." He introduced the girl and announced that she worked at nearby Freestone winery.

"Do you want a round of beers?"

"I'm okay, thanks," she said.

"Nicolas, what are you having?"

"A Stella."

"Okay, I'll be back." I ordered a couple beers from inside the pub. The place was packed and it was barely six o'clock. Nicolas had told me that it was open mic night, but it looked like entire bands were lined up to have their slot. I came back out with two pints and sat next to Nicolas.

"So, how's working for Freestone?" I asked her.

"I really like it. You're at Hirsch?"

"Yeah," I said, sipping the Stella.

"Nice. I was just telling Nicolas that we hired seven interns for harvest at Freestone."

"Seven interns, dude," Nicolas laughed. "Can you believe that?" He was getting socially touchy with her already, like only international types seem to pull off in style. She was loving it—until a mechanic-looking fella showed up and embraced her. She introduced us to her boyfriend as "her new friends." He didn't seem to be particularly thrilled about his girlfriend sitting with a forward Argentinean and a desperate mountain man, so they went inside to meet up with some mutual ones.

Nicolas and I caught up on things. It'd been a year since I'd seen him, when I spent the night at his condo during the Insider's Guide to Dry Creek Valley media and trade conference. At the time, my stomach condition had arisen anew and rifled well out of control; I puked not only at their house mid-way through dinner, but all throughout the media luncheon and out the side of Trevor's truck during the barrel tasting. It was the worst bout of it ever, and I dry heaved upon the hour throughout the long, shaky, hallucinogenic drive back to San Luis Obispo. Nicolas had been concerned and gave me this South American tonic to take, but it didn't work. Nothing did when I hit that point in the game.

"So how's it going?" I changed the subject. "Where's Amber?"

He went into how he and his wife bought a condo at the worst possible time and how they have zero social life in Sonoma. Sounded like my ex and I when we lived in Orange County. I leered often during the evening, from the tan, blue-eyed girl next to us with the furry armpits, to the semi-gothic red head in her late thirties, all done up in stockings and heels from another era.

"I bet she's got black lacy panties on," I said, interrupting the ballad of inflated mortgages. He stopped talking to look at the redhead.

"Well, that would be very nice," he confirmed in that innocent accent of his before laughing.

I didn't have much to tell him about in regards to romance. Other than hooking up with Mary again before moving, and the juicy tale of a girl I met from Santa Cruz over the summer who turned up a few weeks later on Bastille Day in San Luis Obispo with an old bottle of Williams Selyem and an overnight agenda, I was a rolling stone. He mentioned his wife's longboard and that all he needed was a wetsuit and we could try to surf on a Sunday. More musicians poured in for the open mic night. My guitar and harmonica were in the truck, but this was a white reggae funk scene, as far as I could tell. If prompted, I could play "I Know You Rider" and "Pancho and Lefty," but I wasn't feeling it quite yet.

"Hey Nicolas, we'll get up there on stage and play two songs off the *Evita* soundtrack, and after the crowd sees the tears streaming down your face, we'll pass the hat."

"If you would like to bring your nuts onto the stage, by all means do that. But I will not be with you."

"Not even for 'Don't Cry For Me, Argentina'?"

We parted ways out front, and he told me to call him Sunday so he could give me some clonal selections of wines from a Sonoma Coast vineyard to try. Since nobody at his work was a wine nerd like he was, he was allowed to take home interesting bottles. I unlocked my truck thinking about how young married life in California—hell, anywhere—is fucking tough.

CHAPTER 18

On Sunday afternoon, after making up my lunch for the next three days, I brewed some Rooibos tea, chilled a Talley Rosemary's Vineyard Chardonnay and sprawled out and read the *LA Times* on my bed, listening to some of the Thelonious Monk I burned off David's discs. A couple hours into it, I heard some creaking on my front porch, followed by a knock. Assuming it was David, I took a look around to make sure the paraphernalia was out of sight, then I opened up the door to reveal a bearded, afro'd teenager with a stony grill.

"Hey, Darren? I'm Luke. David wanted me to come over 'cause he said you're a musician too."

This was David's teenage son who played bass and lived in Portland, Oregon. I'd heard he was going to spend a little time at the ranch before going off to school.

"Hey Luke, what's up?" I shook hands with him and invited him in immediately. My shuffle on the laptop had switched over to a Wu Tang Clan song, and I had a loaded French press full of dark roast coffee.

"You want some coffee?" I asked him.

"Oh yeah. Really? I'd love to have some coffee."

I pulled out the red chair at my desk for him and then grabbed an extra mug. He was a big kid, a little on the chubby side. In high school we would have nicknamed him "mutant baby" for sure. I didn't see much of a resemblance to David.

"My dad drinks espresso, but only in the morning," he said as I pressed it and poured off two cups.

"I have soy milk and honey if you need it."

"Nah, I'll just drink it black."

"Nice. Me too."

He was looking at my array of stringed instruments, telling me about the huge electric guitar amplifier that was mysteriously in the two large cardboard boxes by the door. He started opening them up, then he and I pulled out a four-speaker stack and a head for it. He used to play death metal in this cottage with a friend, as well as some free form metal-jazz with a trumpet player. Once the boxes were out of the way, I saw the massive chunk taken out of the wall by the door.

"How's that?" I asked him, pointing at what looked like a fist had punched through.

"Oh yeah. My dad wasn't happy about that."

"I might be leaving my own in here by the end of harvest."

We drank our dark roast and I asked him about things, like how long he was here for, what Portland was like. He'd just flown in from a summer camp in the woods of Canada, and he was assuming he and his father were going to spend their week together in San Francisco, going to baseball games and flashy restaurants. But David had picked him up in SF and rushed him right back to the ranch to help with bottling all week. Luke wasn't thrilled. He looked about ten years older than 18.

* * *

On the first morning of bottling week, Barbara and I began sanitizing at six a.m. We started by circulating proxy in the hoses that would flow the wine from our two holding tanks into the bottling truck and eventually the bottle. The plan was to bottle half of the Bohan Dillon Pinot Noir first, which was in two large holding tanks, as well as what was still in barrel and needed to be racked into those tanks once there was enough room to combine everything. That move was going to be tricky.

It turned out our little air pump wasn't going to jive with Jake's bottling system, so we had to use Jake's more industrial pump. Pumping period wasn't welcome at Hirsch or at a lot of wineries that specialize in delicate expensive Pinot Noir, but it had to happen in this case. Mick was skeptical about using Jake's pump. He asked Jake if it was clean already, and Jake said it was. Mick told Barbara and I to sanitize it anyhow. When we hooked our hoses up to it to circulate sodium percarbonate through it, a massive red cloud of residual Drew

Pinot Noir filled up the lines and darkened our water.

"You see?" Mick shouted. "Circulate proxy in that pump for thirty minutes minimum!" he told us. "I hope Jason Drew's a clean winemaker," he warned Jake.

The vineyard crew showed up around eight a.m. to assist, as did Greg the vineyard intern, Luke, and Marie. We were running behind with the pump fiasco, but finally we were all connected and the bottling began. Mick put me on the duty of plastic wrapping the stacked pallets of new wine and forklifting them over to the far end of the crush pad. Luke conveniently assumed the least physically demanding role of stickering the case boxes as they shot down the ramp, leaving poor Greg to lift and stack 40-pound cases of wine for eight hours.

I was on the forklift all afternoon and in charge of pulling out the unsecured cases of wine on a pallet and then shrink-wrapping them, putting placards on the stacks, numbering each full pallet, then moving them to where Barbara's husband loaded them up for transport to David's cold storage warehouse in Santa Rosa. It was a lot to keep track of, but I thrived in the face of the challenge. My hands retained a round, reddened imprint, circularly roasted from the brown roll in the middle of the plastic wrap that I feverishly unraveled around each pallet about ten times. The way you wrap these things confused me at first, even though I'd done it before at Eberle winery. Mick gave me a rapid demo on the first one, but I was missing a vital part of it. Mick was small talking with Luke when he saw my botched wrap job on one of the pallets full of wine and looked at me and raised his hand.

"Yeah?" I asked.

"I have a question?" he said. "What are you doing here?"

"Is it wrong?" I asked.

"Give it to me," he said, motioning toward the roll of plastic. He took it and spun it around the pallet, starting with a knot around the wood, wrapping from bottom to the top, then doing these manic X's up and down the sides to a final, complete wrap. The part I was screwing up on was when you skip one of the sides, and then start painting the second part of the X. I got it then and did a tight, excellent job on the next ones. He made me hold out my hand for a catechistic slap and returned to the cellar.

"I'm gonna have to hire you to wrap my Christmas presents this year!" David exclaimed when he saw one of my better wrap jobs.

* * *

"You know what's really nice after a hard day's work like this?" Luke asked Greg and I while the line was going.

"A woman?" I replied.

Greg snickered in spite of his sweating and resentment he held toward the kid's lazy ways. Luke smiled.

"Well, that too. But really, what's the best after a hard day's work?"

"What?" I asked him.

Greg listened in on this progeny of a California Grand Cru proprietor, pulling another heavy case off the shoot and stacking it on the pallet begrudgingly.

"A nice, big bong rip," Luke answered.

"Yeah?" I still played it innocent.

"Oh yeah."

"I don't think D. Hirsch would appreciate that," I mentioned.

"Pffft," he replied.

Once we finished up our 27th bottled pallet of Bohan Dillon Pinot Noir, David called it a day and let the vineyard crew go. Luke got his sweatshirt and came up to me to basically see if I got high and if I wanted to later.

"Where, though?" I asked.

"You know that big fan in your cabin? That one works pretty good at getting the smoke out."

"Hmm. I don't know." Moments later I comprised an idea. "What if we drive into Guerneville for pizza?" His hairy face beamed.

"Really? You'd drive?"

"Yeah, sure."

"I don't think I can go. I don't have any money. I have a check I need to cash, but it's in pounds."

"Whatever. You can get me back before you leave this weekend."

"No, no. I need to have it be my own money. Let me see if my dad will give me any."

He did just that, and I saw him asking David for cash. Then he came back and said that he had money, but I had the feeling there was lots of sanitizing to be done still, with Barbara and me bound to put in one more exhausting hour. And that's exactly what was on deck. We had to sanitize the hoses again, then Mick wanted us to sanitize the bottling line's pump which was outside. We also had to pour two buckets of leftover wine from the pump into a 5 gallon carboy, gas that, then fill a couple forklift propane tanks for the next morning. It took us to the 7:15 mark, clocking in nearly 13 intense hours with only one

30 minute break.

Luke kept calling the winery phone line from down at his dad's, wondering when I was getting off to take him into Guerneville for pizza. Mick handed me the phone and I told Luke I'd be down soon, that I needed a shower, and that I'd call over to their house when I was ready to leave. An hour later, he happily joined me in the truck, like he'd never had access to much transportation out here at the ranch, and we started the bumpy early evening ride down Bohan Dillon Road toward civilization.

"I couldn't get any," he sadly announced about his plan of getting some weed.

"No biggie," I said, reaching under my seat and pulling out my mason jar.

"Whoa! Man!" his eyes lit up as if he'd never seen so much. I packed my pipe and handed it to him.

"This is really good quality." I mentioned the strain and he took the first rip-roarin' hit and passed me back the pipe with saliva all over it. I dabbed it off and puffed some, and we kept that thing going all the way down to Fort Ross Road, where Luke announced that he was really stoned and asked me if I was okay to drive. It caught me off guard.

"Yeah, of course."

I put on The Band's *Music from Big Pink*. "Your dad has this on vinyl," I said.

"Pizza is gonna be so good," he replied with a red face and wild, hungry eyes.

"Oh yeah?" I was amused at the juvenile stoner speak. It'd been many years since I'd gotten that way about smoking. "So, what are you going to order?" I egged him on, smirking because we were still 45 minutes away from town.

He went on to elaborate on four possible pizza combinations in imaginative detail, including half and half variations and sauce preferences. Then he looked over at me seriously.

"Maybe they'll sell me a beer."

"I was gonna say, with that much facial hair do you ever get carded?"

He told me about times when he was able to order pints in restaurants up in Portland.

We dropped into Guerneville and pulled up alongside Andorno's—a pizzeria Mick had recommended ("great crust" was how he put it). It was after eight o'clock, and, once inside, we found two friendly, older women working the empty place. Luke was entering a heavenly domain, and we swiftly ordered. I asked for a pint of Anchor Steam and Luke quickly added "Sure, I'll do one too" from behind me. We posted up at a table along the wall, and I started talking with the women about their pizzeria, my mom's pizzeria and how they do things. Luke was in complete stoned silence, and we drank our pints quietly. A couple stony locals came in for their takeout pies. One guy in a flannel was so high and out of it that I told Luke, "That dude makes you look sober." We demolished our pizza and thanked the friendly ladies.

Stepping into the warm early evening, I mentioned that we'd have to pick up a pint of Häagen Dazs to take back to the ranch.

"Oh man! That'd be sooo good." Then he felt his pockets and snapped. "No! Oh no! I don't have any money!"

We got into my truck and started driving toward the Safeway parking lot. "You can get me back by the end of the week, man. It's cool."

"Really? I will. Seriously, I will."

In the brightly lit Safeway, we grabbed our pints and Luke disappeared, only to emerge at the checkout stand behind me with napkins and a spork.

"You're gonna kill that thing off here?" I asked him about the pint in his hand. "Aren't you?"

"No. I'll wait till I get back to the house."

"I can't wait, man."

Driving back toward the ranch, I listened to a mix of classic rock and the sounds of Luke viciously slurping his way through that pint of ice cream, obliterating it before we even hit Cazadero proper. Mine was still chilling in a plastic bag.

"How was that thing?" I asked him as he tossed his pint and spoon on the floorboard.

"That was the best," he said with a goofy, sugarcoated smile. As we approached the darkened winery he said, "Can I leave the trash in your car?"

"That might be a good idea. Walking back into the house with an empty pint of ice cream is pretty obvious."

"I know!"

I pulled up at the gate, and he asked me to kill the headlights as he closed the gate behind the truck and got back in. We rambled down the drive and parked. He got out and bee-lined it to the house with his head down, eager to hit the bunk beds without waking up his father.

CHAPTER 19

The next morning, while Barbara and I were sanitizing the hoses for the day's bottling, David shimmied into the cellar with a gracious grin on his face.

"Hey Darren! Your new buddy really had a great time last night. Thanks for taking him out. We don't have the time to do it, so it meant a lot to Marie and me."

"No problem, David."

"Marie and I want to have you down for dinner tonight. Say seven or so?"

Mick overheard this and eyeballed us.

"Really? Cool."

We started the bottling off with the Chardonnay from two smaller portable tanks. A couple hours into it, Jake asked me if we were getting close to empty on the Chardonnay, so I skeptically followed the line into the cellar to see how much Chard remained in the two tanks. As the cellar door closed behind me, I saw Mick on his knees on a top row of barrels in there, racking the remaining barrels of Bohan Dillon Pinot Noir by himself into the larger tanks, now that there was room. He stressfully looked at me with something akin to hatred.

"Jake asked me to check on how much Chard is left," I said.

He just looked at me. I then crawled up the sketchy ladder and saw a shallow pool of cloudy Chardonnay being pumped out of the tank. Not good.

"It's gettin' close!"

"Well tell him!" Mick shouted, pressure releasing a barrel with his face all twisted. I ran outside and told Jake to cut it.

A little while later, David was plowing away on the forklift and I was shrink-wrapping and using the pallet jack to move away the fully-wrapped pallets of wine. David asked me where Mick was.

"He's racking the rest of the Bohan Dillon Pinot in the cellar."

He got off the forklift and yelled, "Darren, this is all yours now!" I took his place on the forklift and continued to bring the empty glass pallets up to the guys in the bottling truck, as well as sticking with my original wrap-and-pull-away job. David came out a few minutes later.

"I highly suggest we don't bother Mick while he's in there racking," he said with a smirk.

At lunch, I gave Luke a ride down to David's. Once at the house, Luke said David was headed down right behind us and Luke would let me know when we had to head back. I sautéed some pasta and ten minutes later heard David's truck pull away without a word. Luke hung back. I brewed us a French press, since he'd been complaining all morning about a dour lack of caffeine. He came to get me at 12:45, announcing that he'd just picked up the phone and it was his dad yelling *We're working down here! Where the hell are you guys?* He inhaled his mug of coffee as we hauled ass back to resentment. I received the silent look of death from Mick, and Luke got the equivalent from his father, since we both waltzed back in together to an intense bottling line scene with David and Mick struggling in our positions. We'd been gone a total of 35 minutes.

I was sweating, working my ass off again. Mick was on a mission, and luckily back inside by himself racking the rest of the Bohan Dillon Pinot into tanks for the next day's bottling. We bottled 350 cases of Chardonnay and more of the unlabeled "M" blend of Pinot Noir. While the line was in full swing, David caught a big frog inside the storeroom, walked out and said, "Hey Luke! Catch!" and he tossed it at his son. Luke ducked like his dad was chucking a snake at him. The frog was big and nervous, but wouldn't leave the bottling line area.

I was excited about dinner at the Hirsch's. I asked Luke what wines he thought his dad was going to open.

"He has a bunch of Bollinger Champagne. Like a Margaret Thatcher one, some other ones. Oh, he really has a bunch of Montrachet."

"Damn. You think he'd open a Montrachet?"

"It's my favorite," Luke said. "I don't know. Hey, Dad!"

Luke approached his dad while he was idling on the forklift by the bottling truck. He leaned in and asked his dad if we were going to be drinking Montrachet at dinner.

"Why drink a truly great wine if you're exhausted?" David replied. He had a point.

Immediately after getting off work, I rushed home and caught the scent of a French bistro coming from David and Marie's. I was filthy and drained. It was honestly the hardest I've ever worked. By multitasking between the forklift duties of feeding the bottling line the pallets of glass, to jumping off and numbering, cinching, wrapping the finished cases and pallet jacking them away, I didn't have much feeling left in my arms and legs. After a quick shower, I snagged a Whitethorn Hyde Vineyard Chardonnay out of the fridge and charged over to their house. I opened the screen door and looked in at Luke seated on the couch with a glass of Chardonnay. His eyes lit up and he waved me in. Once inside the main room, I heard Marie's voice.

"Hello?"

"Hi, Marie."

She smiled at me, then David appeared with a goblet glass of Pinot. His eyes looked more tired than mine.

I handed the bottle of Chardonnay to Marie. "Ooh great, I don't think we've had this."

"Hey ya, Darren," David said, coming over to eagerly look at the bottle. "Is that Hyde?" he asked, putting on his glasses and studying the label. "Oh yeah. No, she makes a Cabernet from—is that Hyde?"

"Yeah, she started making a Cab from Alder Springs Vineyard in Laytonville too."

"Oh really? Up there, huh? You know, everyone really likes their Pinot, but I always liked the Chardonnay from that site."

"Right. I tried a Patz & Hall Pinot from Alder Springs but wasn't too into it. Tasha was making a Cab and Merlot blend that was pretty insane." Her wine from that rocky, northern Mendocino vineyard needed years of bottle age, unless you're a fan of tannins that strip your mouth of all its juices.

"Well, how about some of *our* Chardonnay?" Marie asked me, then laughed. "That'd be great." David, Luke and I sat in the living room while Marie finished making dinner. David threw the restaurant awards issue of *Wine Spectator* across his lap.

"Uh oh, the *Spectator*," I goaded him. Most winery owners that I'd met had a love it or hate it opinion of the magazine, and I was curious about David's take on it. Marie put out a charcuterie platter and handed me a nice glass of Hirsch Chardonnay, fresh off the bottling truck. David said he used to subscribe, then we got onto the subject of selling wine in tasting rooms versus mailing lists. Apparently the neighbors in this part of the Sonoma Coast banned any wine tasting rooms from opening up, so David had a small mailing list of customers that bought wine upon release, but, in light of bottling all of this wine from a bumper crop year, was going to need a lot more of them. Soon it was time for dinner.

David told Luke where to sit at the table, and then sat down himself with both a bottle of red and white. He held out the bottles and said, "Like they used to say, we've got two types of music here: country and western. We've got red and white wine."

The roast chicken and peas were served and Marie, worried that the chicken was overcooked, asked everyone about it. I could've de-feathered and grinded a live one I was so deliriously hungry and tired. We started off in silence for the most part, eating away and drinking both the Hirsch Chardonnay and the M Pinot Noir.

"David, are you okay?" Marie asked him.

"Yeah, I'm fine. I'm so tired I can't tell the difference." A pause. "Are *you* okay?" he fired back.

"Yes, I'm okay."

"Okay then."

"But is the chicken okay?"

"Yes. Yes. The chicken's okay."

Luke rolled his eyes at me. Marie looked at me and said, "This is how every night goes."

"Wow, this is so different," Marie said after tasting the Whitethorn. David and I rinsed our glasses out, and then he poured up a glass of Tasha's Chardonnay and passed me down the bottle.

"Oh, what a gorgeous nose on it," he said. I got to that level with them and smelled pears, green apples, oak, the yeasty note of lees, and then tasted it. All that bright Meyer lemon zing that I'd remembered in this wine had sort of faded away, making the wine rich and lush, but on its way out.

"Do you like hers or ours better?" David presented that loaded question to his wife.

"Ours," she said.

"Yeah, me too. I mean, this is a great wine. This is an excellent wine."

Luke decided to join in on the white wine criticism and loaded his glass with it while David was talking. David eyeballed his son.

"Hey, easy there, Luke. That's not root beer, you know."

Luke got physically irritated. "I know!" He handed the bottle back to his dad.

We drank and ate, and soon I'd moved on to the M blend.

"So have you decided on what to call this?" I asked. Mick and I had talked about it earlier. It was really expensive to bottle wines without labels, since you'd have to open the cases at a later date and run them through the assembly line again when you ultimately printed them. The blend could have stayed in barrel for a later bottling, but it was important for us to make cellar space for the forthcoming harvest and to have empty barrels to use for the new wine. Hence the "shiner" bottles of mystery.

David looked at me with confusion, then said matter-of-factly, "It's the 'M'; that's what it is."

"Remember my idea for it?" Luke interjected, talking about his drawing or something for a label.

Then the wine or my delirium prompted me to mention the movie *Ghost Dog*. "I think the movie poster for *Ghost Dog* with Forrest Whitaker and his gun with that silencer on it, right on the label. That'd be cool."

David laughed out loud and said, "I am so thrilled to hear somebody else loves that film as much as me."

"Oh, Dad," Luke started excitedly, "I'm goin' to see the Wu-Tang—"

"I mean, the part where it talks about a hawk that marks its bird in the midst of a thousand birds, and pursues it… I mean, that is it!"

David snapped on Luke later when he used the word "dude" while talking about the summer camp he just came back from. As the second course of salad was finished, and then the sorbet, David was rubbing his eyes in exhaustion.

"What did you think about the chicken?" Marie still really wanted to know.

"How about another bottle of wine?" David said.

"I wouldn't turn it down," I said, raising my eyebrows at Luke.

David got up and walked out onto the back deck and down the steps to an area beneath his dining room. The cellar. I'd read about some wine writers who came out here and were entertained with a tasting of six of David's favorite wines from his vineyard. There was a shot of David in his cellar on that website pulling out a bottle, but I hadn't seen the underground room yet. I'd heard it— the whirring of the cooling fan in the mid-day heat. Luke had mentioned that his dad only really spends money on three things: eating at good restaurants, music, and wine. Sometimes he'll order a whole bottle for himself at a restaurant, and if anyone at the table says anything, he'll say "What? It's a great wine!"

He emerged from the cellar with a Chinon rouge. He said it was 100% Pinot Noir as he uncorked and poured it off.

"They do Pinot there too?" I asked later as we tasted it. "I thought Cab Franc was the only red of Chinon?"

"You know, let me see," and he grabbed his huge Barnes and Noble "Wine" book and looked it up. "No no, they grow some Pinot. I really trust Kermit Lynch."

"The importer?"

"I buy up nearly anything he offers me. He's fantastic."

"I'm gonna throw on some music," Luke announced.

"Yeah, how about a little Carter Family," David suggested.

Marie was doing the dishes and mentioned that the Carter Family wasn't a good idea. Luke put on Medeski, Martin and Wood and returned. We talked some more, but David was even more beat than I was, and I remembered I had Mary showing up that night; she was interviewing across the ridge at Seaview Winery the next day and needed a place to stay. Female company in this worn out condition was foolish, especially with a six a.m. start time.

"Why don't you guys carry on," he said with a yawn. "I'm gonna get some sleep."

"All right, thanks for everything," I said. It was ten 'til nine.

David walked over to Marie, and they exchanged some words. Then David said, "You know, Marie's gonna go to bed too. So maybe that's not the best idea."

I looked at Luke and said, "You wanna come up to my place?"

David disappeared. I thanked Marie for dinner, then waited for Luke by his old bedroom while he searched for his iPod. There were two old bunk beds in there. He'd said he slept on the bottom one because he didn't think the top one would support him anymore. He grabbed the iPod and we started toward the door, but were met by a disoriented David Hirsch. Without glasses, tousled hair and a pair of custom, button-up boxer shorts that looked like they dated back to the Appalachian era of The Carter Family, he was unrecognizable. His furry belly glistened out before him. It tripped me out to see this Pinot phenomenon in the near nude. He put his hand out for a parting shake and we headed up to the cottage.

I'd missed a call from Mary during dinner, but didn't call her back. I poured Luke some more of the Whitethorn Chard that Marie had returned, and I grabbed the pipe and packed it. He fiddled around on my guitar, then we smoked, and I finally got a repeat call from Mary, who was obviously lost on the way here. We tried to help on the phone, but she became even more lost. A very cooked Luke Hirsch sauntered home around 11.

A half hour later, Mary called me from up by the winery, two hours late and ready for me to meet her there and lead her back. Half wasted in the Tacoma, I tried to take off in a loose patch of dirt but kept getting stuck going uphill. Just what David wanted to hear in a Chinon-lipstained slumber outside his bedroom window after a day of bottling hell. I swerved out of it and drove up through the gate toward the winery.

I didn't see her truck up there, so I did a U-turn and idled out front. She pulled up from behind and idled alongside the passenger side of my truck. I was grouchy, drunk and stoned. She seemed hesitant and sorry, rolling down her window and quietly anticipating some wrath on my part. I gave her a small taste of it.

"Are you kidding me?" I said. Her face didn't change, and she said nothing. "Here, follow me!" I took off, and within seconds I was feeling like shit for saying that to her. By the time we were parked and getting out of our trucks, I apologized and made good. She was nearly in tears over it all. Her reddish brown hair was long and smelled good as I hugged her. She still seemed like a college girl to me, with her smile and girlish, freckly face. I led her into the cottage and poured her a glass of Chardonnay. There was only one chair and a bed in there, so I laid back as she talked about how lost she actually was, having missed the crucial right turn onto Fort Ross Road and continuing north to Annapolis almost. I couldn't stop yawning then in my mental and physical exhaustion. She took a shower and I got into bed, passing out well before she was drying off.

* * *

I had a second bad dream—two nights in a row. This one starred my friend Nicolas, but instead of a winery job, he worked at a Chevron gas station in San Luis Obispo near the Edna Valley. He wasn't happy with his job. The Chevron used to be a full service station, but was pretty gutted out. After visiting for a bit, Larry, the old trippy guy who really works at a Shell Beach gas station, came out of the bathroom, and I said "Hey, Larry." Then, once outside, I noticed smoke and a fire behind the Chevron and saw smoke rising up in the field right behind the station. "Nicolas!" I alerted him. "There's a fire roaring right into the station!" I pointed, and soon we were running to gather up our things and take off. Old Larry didn't believe us at all, but instead threatened Nicolas for leaving on the clock. For some reason, my belt was off and in the back room of the gas station. It was important enough for me to run in looking for it and I barely got out alive as the flames hit the back of the station. The whole thing ignited in flames moments later, Larry and all.

CHAPTER 20

After a successful week of bottling and cleaning up empty barrels, I was ready to cut loose. Our crew was so efficient we finished up a day early, meaning the bottling truck and crew were able to take off mid-day Thursday. David and Mick were in high spirits. Jake mentioned to Mick that they wouldn't be able to work up at Hirsch again, citing something about nearly dying in the semi on the way up one of the roads. Future mobile bottlings would have to be done by a company with a much smaller truck.

I'd originally planned on eating the chocolate-covered mushroom that Mary had gifted me, but with the recurring bad dreams of the week and the stressful energy passed down to me from the workplace, I decided against it. I'm sure the last thing the Hirsch family would've liked to find is my spun-out corpse lying face down in the dirt on Bohan Dillon Road being ripped apart by buzzards.

On Saturday morning—after sleeping for close to 11 hours—I started arranging a shindig at the ranch. David, Marie and Luke were off to San Francisco. Trevor had called a couple times saying he had money now and wanted to come back, possibly with Leslie. He also mentioned that some mutual friends of ours, Nate and Clarissa, were in Santa Rosa and that Nate wanted to see Hirsch. I called Nate afterward and invited him up to camp and provided the directions to the vineyard. After haggling for 15 minutes with Trevor about picking me up the weekend *San Francisco Chronicle*, I told him on the phone that whoever got up here first was going to drink the only bottle of Hirsch Pinot I owned. He was bringing Grace back up for sure, but they were just waiting on Leslie to get off work. As a true only child, Trevor was absolutely livid about the possibility of arriving late and missing the Pinot.

"Bro, the only thing Nate is going to drink when he gets there is a French press of coffee. He can't hang. He'll pass out before we even get there." I knew Trevor was more concerned with missing out on the good juice than Nate's issue of having alcohol hit him like barbiturates. We got off the phone, and a half hour later Trevor called me to sweetly confirm that he got me the paper and ask if he could bring me anything else.

"You're the biggest only child I know," I said to him. I made sure Trevor clarified the sleeping arrangements up here, especially in light of six grown adults and the fact that Nate and Clarissa weren't in a camping mood at all. Of course I wouldn't have minded, but I didn't want to imply that I expected Leslie to sleep with me if she came here. The more I thought about it and how I'd pursued her weeks back at Trevor's with the Monthélie and the serenade, I decided I'd be low profile this time, and if she had a change of heart and wanted me in that regard, her taking the offensive would be the only way things were going to happen.

"See ya around six," Trevor said.

I spent that morning up at the winery on the computer after closing the cellar's roll up doors for Mick as he had requested over the phone.

"I really appreciate it, Darren," a mellow, at-home Mick said. Come afternoon, I strummed and sipped on a Guigal St. Joseph Blanc on the deck at David and Marie's while the Littorai-heavy cellar hummed beneath me. The view and the silence from their deck was soul stirring.

As expected, and much to Trevor's chagrin, Nate and Clarissa arrived first, so I drove up and met them at the winery. Nate was an old surfing buddy I'd met through Trevor in Santa Cruz years beforehand, and he was now obsessed with wine. Knowing this, I showed them through block six. Nate snapped some pictures while Clarissa gripped his hand through the rows, terrified of the rattlesnakes.

Back at the cottage, I'd made a plate of grapes, carrots and Gruyere; we took it to the patio with the rest of the Guigal and the first of the Bohan Dillon Pinot. I suggested to Nate that we take a phone picture of him drinking it with the label in view to send to Trevor. He did. Soon a cold wind propelled by the marine layer crept up onto the ridge, and with a couple glasses of wine in each of us, we went back to the cottage. I started getting dinner ready—egg flower soup and soy-ginger tofu couscous with cauliflower simmering on the stove. It was mellow hanging out with just Nate and Clarissa. I asked about her friend they'd introduced me to over the summer in Santa Cruz, the one that turned up at my house on Bastille Day. Clarissa shared that the girl really liked me and that she was already talking about coming up to see me at Hirsch.

After dark, Trevor and the girls barged in and the vibe surged to a rowdy level. Within seconds, Grace was plugging her vaporizer in like she was an electric guitarist who showed up late to play the gig. Clarissa's eyes widened. Trevor started popping bottles. We rapid-fire tasted through about six wines. I served bowls of soup on my little round coffee table with everyone crowded around. Trevor grabbed the Schramsberg Blanc de Blancs that Leslie had brought and said, "Ever heard a nun fart?" as he slowly popped the cork. The tight squeak of the disgorgement made us all laugh.

We ate, drank, laughed, got high, and then, around midnight, Grace asked me to play a song I had written. Trevor drunkenly backed her up.

"Come on! Let's hear 'Fishsticks Fridays'!"

I'd made the mistake of forwarding Trevor the link to a self-written song about my childhood, at Grace's request. Properly titled "Fishstick Fridays," the song captured a chunk of my childhood though three simple acoustic verses in the lyrical form of instructions to the legions of female babysitters that watched my brother and I. It's essentially the blues of the children of restaurant people. The opening line goes, "Dear Melinda, there's fishsticks in the freezer, mac and cheese on the counter, and the laundry needs to be transferred." It was only a matter of time before Trevor rousted me about it, since indie folk was the last genre you could find him listening to.

"All right, it's an outdoor gig though. Let's go." I put on my harmonica and grabbed the guitar. Nate and Clarissa, who'd been fading fast, stayed in to set up a makeshift sleeping area on the kitchen floor beside my bed. I'd marketed the wood floor space of the bathroom as being the suite of choice, but they weren't having it. They could've fallen asleep by nine, especially after the fourth bottle of wine.

Trevor opened up his truck and started blasting Damian Marley in the bright, star-glistening night. Grace put on a devilish grin and started hullahooping with her Rasta-colored custom hoop. Leslie smoked a cigarette and hung out, but by no means had she and I flirted or even gotten closer than my hug hello. Nate and Clarissa managed to come outside for a bit, with Nate's arms wrapped around Clarissa from behind, trying to groove her to the reggae, but she was done and off they went into my cottage.

"I dig the pre-show music," I told Trevor, holding my guitar, giving him the signal that we were out there because I was asked to play a song, not to hear Junior Gong under the stars.

He quietly nodded at Grace as she sensually writhed her hips within the hoop. In a sex-fueled trance, he leaned in close and said in all seriousness, "Bro, just look at that." He had a point.

"Six times on Friday," he cryptically added, with his eyebrows raised in astonishment.

She stopped hullahooping and said, "Let's hear it!" She told Trevor to kill the Marley, which he did with reluctance.

"Okay," I said, Leslie and Grace staring at me "This first song I'm gonna dedicate to Trevor."

"Oh really?" Trevor said, putting his arm around me with intimidation in mind.

"It's a Willie Nelson song called 'All the Soft Places to Fall.'" I sang the first verse and chorus, but after the line "the women I've known have been many," Trevor reached inside his truck and blasted Junior Gong again.

"Okay, this crowd sucks, I'm going off stage," I said, storming off.

"Aww," Grace said as I started toward the cottage.

"Delmore, are you really going to bed?" Leslie surprisingly called out to me in P.E. coach fashion.

"Yeah," I said, going into the cottage and trying not to step on Nate and Clarissa. I heard Leslie following me. I went into the bathroom and closed the door. After brushing my teeth, I opened the door to find Leslie waiting to use it after me.

"Hey, you don't have to sleep on the floor."

"Thank you," she said with a nervous laugh.

"I won't attack you like Trevor and Grace would or anything."

The duo had apparently made repeated three-way requests to her the whole way out here. She went into the bathroom as I got into bed. Moments later she joined me. I kept my distance, but I could still smell the trace of cigarette smoke on her lips. She small-talked about how weird it was that Nate and Clarissa chose to sleep right there, inches away, instead of behind the closed door of the bathroom. Then she cuddled up to me, so I put my right arm up around her and soon our faces were within an inch of each other. I could feel her heart beating, then I found her lips with mine and kissed her. This time she was ready for it, which meant she had finally broken it off with her boyfriend, or else the setting and my vegetarian cooking took things up a notch. Regardless of the inspiration, we were going at it. She giggled at how close Nate and Clarissa were to us. We could hear mutual snoring going on, so after she removed her tank top, I undid her bra and felt her and kissed her breasts and her neck, gripping the back of her head and bringing her in for a round of open-mouthed kisses. I pressed against her, and she gasped with the connection. I wanted to be closer, so I kneeled back and began to pull her pajama bottoms off, but she laughed and held on to them. She pulled me in close.

"We can't fuck with Nate and Clarissa right there," she said.

"I know, but we can do other things, right?" She smiled and off came her bottoms.

"You're driving me crazy," she whispered.

My heart was roaring as I licked and sucked on her chest and kissed my way down her abdomen. I ventured a finger inside of her and she gasped. I left it there and kissed her belly button ring. I ventured further but she stopped me.

"No, you can't," she said. "Not with them right there. Come here." She pulled my face back up to hers and we kissed for awhile. I eventually let up and mellowed out, laying on my back with her head on my chest and my arm cradled around her. We fell asleep that way.

In the morning, she separated herself far away from me when Trevor came in to use the bathroom.

* * *

Thanks to Nate, who fulfilled my request for eggs and bacon, we were able to cook up a feast for breakfast on Sunday. He and Clarissa had to get going before it was done, so only the four of us plowed through a couple French presses and the *San Francisco Chronicle*, with the vaporizer plugged in and reggae music going. Even though he bragged incessantly about the "epic sex" he had under the stars, Trevor was suspicious of Leslie and I and was being short with her in front of us. He kept staring at her all morning with this serious look on his face until she laughed nervously about it and told him to stop. He obviously still had a heavy crush on her, no matter how "mind-blowing" he made Grace out to be.

Before they left, I got Leslie's number and hugged her goodbye. I shook hands with Trevor and hugged Grace as well, who bagged up her vaporizer and got into the truck. They drove up the dirt road to the gate, and Leslie hopped out to open it and let them through. The sound of their engine faded out. With a lukewarm, unfiltered coffee in my hand, I sat on the tailgate of my truck in the sun in silence. I didn't think the evening was going to end like it did. Maybe this place enamored everyone who visited it. I'd shared my bed with two girls in one week, way out in the middle of nowhere.

I checked my phone and saw a missed call from Mary the evening before. It made me feel guilty. If she did get the job a mile away from here, she'd want a relationship. It's fair to assume that I was a major motivation for her quitting her job in Santa Barbara and moving to Cazadero. After all, she had bought a townhouse in Santa Barbara and had landed a winemaker position there. For her to leave all of this to accept a step-down position as a temporary assistant in the wilds of the Sonoma Coast didn't make any career sense at all. With increasing options of living out a single life I never knew before marriage and a growing fear of commitment, an exclusive relationship was the last thing I desired. She and I had been through this before, and I'd told her the same line and always felt cruel afterward.

It would be interesting to see if Leslie would ever come back up here to see me, and if she would be with others the next time or alone.

* * *

Around sunset, as I crested Meyers Grade Road with groceries and a bag of fresh laundry on the passenger seat, a massive dark animal emerged from the brush and bolted into the road. Then I saw the snout, tusk and mottled fur and realized it was a beast of a wild boar. I didn't think they got that big, but there it was, and I fucking broadsided it at 40 miles per hour.

"Whoa-ho!" I shouted. My bag of groceries split open. The boar squealed and rebounded, running back behind my truck as I kept going. It was gigantic and seemed to handle the blow. That was until a Ford Explorer behind me with its lights on came into range. In the rearview, I watched as the headlights went up and down twice, running over the massive beast, and then stared as it miraculously tore off into the field. I couldn't believe it. I didn't know whether to stop or to just keep going. As if rattlesnakes and mountain lions weren't enough out here, enter a cow-sized, bulletproof pig. I drove on, eventually laughing at the absurdity and paying attention to the new clicking sound I heard when I turned the wheel to the right.

CHAPTER 21

After sharing my wild boar story with Barbara and Mick the next morning, we split off into different sections of the vineyard to collect grape samples for analysis. It was the week before Labor Day. David had us mainly cruising through the younger vines and clipping cluster samples, since they were known to ripen earlier than the more established, famous blocks. My truck was put to the test out in the teen numbered blocks that faced more easterly toward Marcassin Blue Slide Ridge vineyard. Now knowing the size of the snakes in the vicinity, I got the chills every time I made a pass through a high weed row, charging through the brush as fast as I could.

I knew why Mick had clarified to me how important passion was to this job, because if you didn't care about making a great bottle of wine, you were unsupervised as to whether or not the buckets full of 25 clusters you brought back to the lab for analysis were really from the blocks you said they were from.

Finding the blocks was a nightmare enough, since nothing was numbered out there and there were vineyards within vineyards. I had my clipboard full of maps and my vine and row count sheets, but it took a careful, obsessive eye to make sure you were in the right place. I was amazed at how the fruit in one specific section of the vineyard was looking ready to pick, with birds already dining away at the riper clusters on the outer vines, while other sections a quarter mile away were just starting to turn color.

Back at the lab, Barbara and I switched off on hand-crushing the samples with a potato masher and a strainer into Mick's measuring cups. We'd stick some tape with the vineyard block number on the cup once each was done, then take the skins and stems outside for disposal. The question in the air was whether or not we'd be laboring on the eponymous holiday. Mick's announcement of "Are you guys ready for fruit?" seemed to answer that one for us.

We readied the crush pad for production that week. Mick took the tarps off the red wine steel basket press and got it activated, while Barbara and I rolled out the relic of winemaking past known as Bertha: the yellow, World War II era bladder press that was once used by Williams Selyem and Porter Bass Winery for Chardonnay. Now the old, ugly, hotdog-shaped cylinder was here at Hirsch and looked historical at best. We circulated sodium percarbonate in it and let it sit overnight. We brought out two sorting tables, placing one before the destemmer up top and the other after the destemmer down below. A test run on the destemmer and the tables proved that things were working. The air was thick with anticipation. Harvest was a few more hot days away.

* * *

Two days later, at 5:30 a.m., I heard the rattle of a tractor and people shouting in both Spanish and English. *"Acción!"* I kept hearing in what sounded like Robert De Niro's accent, but I wasn't sure. Day one of harvest at the Hirsch Vineyard was here. They were swiftly picking block nine, which was planted in the hottest bowl on the property. I rose from bed with a knot in my stomach and tightened the cinch with a concentrated cup of French roast.

Barbara welcomed me at the winery with a very serious and cautious "Good morning." Mick simply nodded. He mentioned the grape scale that was plugged in near the roll-up door to the old barrel room. We would be weighing each filled bin on that scale, recording the weights on a clipboard, then stacking the grape bins in the ultra-chilled old barrel room until it was time to process. I learned that if your grapes get too hot after being picked, they'll usually start fermenting immediately, which ruins a decent pre-fermentation cold soak period where most of the color and good flavor extraction from the skins occurs. With Pinot not being the darkest red wine grape out there, a cold soak was important to avoid having your red look like a rosé.

David would pull up honking every hour in his truck with two to four bins of Pinot Noir stacked in it from the field. Whichever one of us wasn't setting up the crush pad for destemming or sanitizing bins, parts, and buckets had to run like hell over to the forklift and unload him. This entailed weighing the fruit, recording the numbers, stacking and parking the bins inside the cellar, and then loading him up with fresh bins for the next load. Barbara warned me to drop everything if I saw David coming with grapes, otherwise he'd get angry about every wasted second and start shouting.

After a frantic 30-minute lunch break, I returned to the winery for the first run of processing.

"*Acción!*" David shouted at the exhausted vineyard crew as the sorting table was fired up. This was it. I had a sanitized half-ton bin in place at the end of the lower sorting table that would collect destemmed grapes from 14 sets of sorting hands. Only the most perfect berry would make it in. Barbara's husband Mike had the first half ton bin of Hirsch Vineyard Pinot Noir clusters up there on the forklift, ready to be side dumped onto the upper sorting table that Mick was standing beside. The vineyard guys, having picked the stuff at the break of dawn, slowly assumed their hand sorting positions.

"You let these guys stand around long enough, they'll go to sleep," David said, standing beside Marie at the mouth of the destemmer. "*Acción!*" he shouted again.

The tiny purple and black skinned grapes had softened with enough sugar and flavor to send a diabetic reaching for the needle. You couldn't help but snack on some here or there. Aside from the vineyard guys, Barbara and Nikki Bohan from the Bohan ranch were by my side. Nikki was around my age with long black hair, and she had married into the Bohan family who farmed their own grapes down the way. She offered to work part-time at Hirsch to make some extra cash. We bent over into each destemmed and sorted half ton bin and pulled out leaves, raisins, and what they call "jacks," which are bright green, miniature stems that the destemmer didn't snag out of there. As soon as each bin was mostly full, I pallet-jacked it away, and the guys threw the next sanitized bin in its place. We were keeping the vineyard blocks separate from field to barrel, so labeling everything was extremely sensitive.

"How are you holding up out here," Nikki asked me, since she had made the permanent move to Cazadero herself and knew well the isolation of her now namesake road.

"It's pretty wild, but I like it," I answered.

"I have tons of movies, so if you want to borrow any, I'll bring some to you. They're all on VHS though!" She laughed about that.

"Classic," I said. "I don't have a TV in my cottage."

"Darren's in the old caretaker's cottage now," Barbara pointed out to her.

We were collectively bending over for hours of sorting until we started seeing imaginary jacks and leaves on everything. It looked like Marie was wearing jacks for earrings. The guys were very quiet, hand sorting, watching how we were hand sorting, and it wasn't until the end of the day after Barbara was trying to chat with them that they loosened up a little. Everardo worked up on top beside Mike and Mick, seeing the fruit of his labor going into the destemmer. Mick was tasting the clusters and chatting while things ran smoothly. He looked like he was having the most fun that I'd ever seen him have here.

Once we were done processing for the afternoon, we began the arduous and sticky clean up process, avoiding drunk yellow jackets and bees and making it look like harvest hadn't hit the equipment yet. Meanwhile, Mick made sulfite additions to each bin and stirred the dissolving powder in with the big stainless steel punch-down rod. We were beat by sundown, which was when Mick fired up the forklift to start side dumping the bins into their clean, respective open-top fermentation tanks.

* * *

On day three of the crush, I found myself cussing out inanimate objects. A leaf or a broom and especially the water hoses. These hoses were out to get me. How they twisted away from me with all their might as I coiled them neatly, how the spray guns on the end would blast me randomly when they slipped out of my hands and hit the crush pad.

I got my first bee sting around three o'clock while we were hand sorting the grapes coming off the lower sorting table into a bin. "Ow," I said matter-of-factly. I pulled my open left palm out of the bin and saw the stinger in my skin. I pulled it right out, and the Tetanus shot-like ache made itself known, then magnified. My hand swelled up, but I could keep working. Mick had mentioned how he's deathly allergic to bees, so when I told him I was stung he had a grave look to him, as this was only the beginning.

David was hell-bent against overripe fruit and the resultant, high-alcohol wines, so the crew was picking a lot of Pinot. It was destined to be another 15-hour day, with a sore, half-hour, anxiety-driven lunch break. I'd been treating myself right as far as my meals were concerned. Mick still didn't phrase it as "take lunch." He'd say "go eat." And eating was becoming the luxury of my days. I crafted a club sandwich on day two and bacon and egg burritos on day three. Somewhere in this newfound delirium, I had decided that it'd be bacon on everything out here.

After lunch, David asked me to thank Mary for the bottle of Santa Rita

Hills Pinot she had given them for allowing her to stay the night while she interviewed at Seaview. Both he and Marie loved that wine apparently.

"I don't usually like central California wine," David said, "but the acid was amazing in it. We couldn't stop drinking it!"

Marie turned up then, dressed like she could've been a roadie for The Clash on their *Combat Rock* tour, complete with military fatigues and a bandanna. I overheard her walk up to David, asking, "Is this appropriate for crushing grapes?"

"Yeah, it's fine sweetheart," he replied. There must have been a little issue over her shorts and tight, sleeveless getup the day before.

The conversational highlight of the day came by way of Barbara while breaking our spines on the hand sorting line. She was talking about when she used to work graveyard shifts at Safeway in Guerneville and how she got so sick of the phone ringing while she slept during the day that she actually put the cordless phone in the refrigerator. This was a major rural confession. Even with Nikki being pretty country herself, she was cracking up about it.

"Oh Barbara," she said, "you really shouldn't have said anything about that."

"I hate my answering machine, too!" Barbara added, starting to get humorously defensive. I nodded and saw some strange practicality in it.

"But why didn't you just unplug the phone?" Nikki asked.

"I don't know! Working those hours makes ya a little crazy."

By 9:30 that night I was feeling strange, spotting Mick as he dumped each bin of grapes into our array of open top tanks. It was hypnotic, seeing how the sulfite additions browned a bit of the red juice in each bin, watching the colors go from pink to brown under the light of the forklift as the juice trickled into the tanks. I was a little weary of doing the bin dumping on the forklift. The arms that we affixed to the forklift were supposed to lock that bin in as it was raised and spun upside down, unloading the destemmed and sorted fruit into the open-top tank, but I've seen bins fly right off before. David would snap if I lost a half-ton of Hirsch Pinot Noir on the concrete.

When I drove away from the winery that night, we had processed the majority of the young vine Pinot from about eight different vineyard blocks. After work, I ate a pasta carbonara with an off dry Anne Amie Viognier from Oregon. I could've drunk the whole bottle in the residual heat of the night. I switched to the going-on-three-nights unlabeled barrel sample of CR88 clone Pinot from Nicolas. Both this and the 667 sample he gave me were incredible. The CR88 was dark and savory, with sage and super cola-accented fruit. Tight wine, maybe too solid, especially since it was still that way on night three. A

Pinot with prostate, if you will.

Even with a couple glasses of wine in me, it was impossible to go to sleep after such a machinated shift. Lying in bed close to midnight, I was on the phone with Nate and Clarissa's friend Heather—the girl that turned up on Bastille Day—and she indeed confirmed her road trip up to Sonoma on Labor Day weekend. She used the same sort of preface that she had when she came to San Luis Obispo, saying that she was mainly going wine tasting but if I'm free that she would like to see me. She was really giggly on the phone and confessed to being most of the way through a Williams Selyem Zinfandel. She added that her boss had set her up with a tasting appointment at Williams Selyem, which was a sought-after winery that rarely did tastings at all. I told her I wanted to go if I had the afternoon free. She said she'd have to ask and kept talking as things went black.

"Hello?" I heard her asking, barely waking me back up.

"Yeah, I'm here," I confirmed. I was absolutely done, and, with my eyes closed, I mumbled for her to come stay the night at Hirsch if she wanted and that I should have Sunday off but couldn't guarantee Monday. "I'll cook for you," I said. "My place is tiny though."

CHAPTER 22

On Saturday evening, I was deep inside one of the larger stainless steel tanks scrubbing the inner wall with liquefied citric acid. We'd processed a lot of grapes all afternoon, and more and more of the winery's tanks were getting filled up with the harvest. It was only supposed to be a nine-hour day according to David, but here Mick, Barbara and I were on the crush pad with at least three more hours left to go.

Mick suddenly stuck his head inside the tank's door and looked up at me.

"Darren, there's a young lady here to see you," he said in an amused, girlish tone before walking away. A bolt of joy rushed through me, though I knew the downside was that it was close to seven o'clock already and twenty-some bins of destemmed Pinot had neither been sulfured nor dumped into tanks. I gave the tank a rinse and climbed out barefoot onto the wet concrete.

I caught sight of Heather standing sheepishly out of everyone's way by a cluster of the smaller tanks that were yet to be filled. David was over there on one knee working on a glycol fitting for one of the tanks. She looked unbelievably attractive at that moment, especially out here, wearing a thin, button-up sweater over a low-cut tank top and tight jeans that accentuated her curves. When her big brown eyes saw me, she gave me a smile. Barbara, Mick and David were having a look as well, and I gave her a tentative hug since I was soaked and filthy.

"I am so happy to see you here," I told her, and it was the truth. "You don't even know."

"Oh my god, look at you," she laughed.

"It's disgusting, right? Hey, do you want to meet David Hirsch?"

She worked for an attorney who collected a lot of Hirsch Vineyard wines and other insanely expensive Sonoma Coast Pinots and Chardonnays, so for her, being here and meeting David himself was like meeting a celebrity. He stood and greeted her formally, with a sweet smile and handshake.

"Oh, hi, Heather, I'm David Hirsch."

I asked permission to take a break and get her settled in the cottage.

"You picked a good night to come here," David assured her. "Darren and the gang should be off pretty soon."

She drove down behind me and I directed her to park out of David and Marie's way on the side of the turnaround. She had a good-sized bag and a few wines from her boss's collection, which she showed off to me as I led her inside. I had zero desire to return to the winery. There was an open bottle of Hirsch Pinot Noir that I'd bought from David in anticipation of this, and I poured her a glass and told her to help herself to anything in the refrigerator. She sat on the edge of the bed and crossed one long leg over the other.

"Feel free to walk around the property," I said.

"I really don't think that will be happening," she laughed. I'd made the mistake the other night of telling her about the snake.

I leaned down and kissed her, and she met me with a deeper, hungrier one.

"I'll be back by nine," I said, forcing myself out the door.

When I pulled back up at the winery, I noticed a new car parked by Mick's trailer and saw Cornelius roaming around. The dog had been gone for a few days but appeared to be back. It was Mick's wife Anne's car, and I was relieved to see that he too had a reason to finish up as soon as possible. I parked and saw her talking to Barbara and Mick. He introduced me to Anne, who was warm and friendly right away. Barbara was clearly starved for another woman to talk to out here.

Mick went over the game plan that would get us out of there by nine, which entailed adding sulfur to the destemmed bins and forklifting them one by one into their appropriate fermentation tanks, then covering the tanks with custom-sewn tops so bugs and other animals couldn't help themselves during the night. Anne took Cornelius back to the trailer, telling Mick that she was going to make him dinner. David told us to have a good rest the next day and got going.

An hour later, as I was spotting Mick again on the dumping, Anne walked back over and said that Cornelius had been sprayed by a skunk. Mick stopped everything and, sure enough, Cornelius came over in a frazzled state and reeked. He was sneezing and madly pawing at his eyes. Apparently he took it right in the face. They had to sleep in that trailer with a dog who smelled like pure musk. Mick began spraying Cornelius off. Selfishly, I was counting the seconds to get back to Heather in the cottage, and this holdup pushed us back to ten p.m. I was furious when I was finally released and got into my truck. I took the road down at breakneck speed and expected Heather to be pissed off and hungry when I arrived. But when I charged into the cottage, she was serene, lying on my bed with her laptop open and listening to Dave Matthews. I couldn't believe it. My ex-wife was so intense that she would have raised pure hellfire over something like this.

"I'm so sorry," I said. "You've gotta be starving."

"I'm fine. Take a shower."

"He kept me there forever, kind of on purpose, in a weird way."

"It's harvest. I expected it."

I washed my body down like a hypochondriac and paused on what to wear. This was technically our third date, but with 400 square feet to work with and nowhere to go, it was pretty obvious what was about to happen. I put on a t-shirt and corduroy pants in the bathroom and opened the door. She was standing in the kitchenette looking for a corkscrew for a chilled bottle of Kistler Chardonnay that she brought along. This must be a dream, I was thinking. It was 10:30 on a distant mountaintop, and this sexy, generous soul was opening a hundred dollar bottle of wine for me.

* * *

I didn't even brake as we passed the winery on Sunday morning as Heather and I fled the ranch. Mick was definitely around, but checking in would have put my dwindling freedom in jeopardy. Heather was wearing a pair of white shorts, and I rested my hand on her smooth, athletic thigh. The night before had put me in a haze of contentment with the laziest of smiles plastered on my face. I pointed out some of the sights of Bohan Dillon Road as we drove in the direction of the Russian River Valley and her appointment at Williams Selyem.

The gate on Westside Road was open for us, and we drove into a tranquil, lonesome property without any vines of its own. There were only two cars parked by the winery itself. I expected similar harvest chaos, but it was a quiet Sunday morning at this place. We ducked into an old building and found the winemaker Bob Cabral inside; he was in his forties, with a sandy mustache and semi-long, blondish hair. The features of his face reminded me a bit of a Matt Groening cartoon character that I couldn't place. Dressed in a t-shirt and jeans, he greeted

Heather with a hug and shook my hand with sincerity.

"Darren is working for Hirsch," Heather mentioned.

"You're working for David?" he asked.

"Yeah. We're full on already."

"Is he taking his meds?" He laughed and then pointed at an open bottle of Pinot on the sink counter by a bunch of lab equipment. "I opened the Weir for you guys. Here, let me pour you a glass." The wine smelled a lot like some of the Hirsch barrel samples from the year before, but had more of a wild cherry and earth aroma and was thicker and more oak rich on the palate. We embarked on a private tour, where he showed us the stall of infamous milk tanks that they used as fermenters for Pinot Noir. They were cylinders that had been cut in half and placed open-top in a row. Five of them were full of destemmed Pinot Noir, and a girl was in there doing punch-downs with a steel rod. I would be doing punch-downs just like her once our tanks became active with fermentation.

I asked about their intern situation. Bob said they had four and they lived in a house they converted into four separate apartments with satellite TV and Wi-Fi. "We're good to them," he said. "By next week, we'll have three shifts going with hourly limits, and everyone gets a minimum of one full day off. We do harvest lunches daily."

"Bob, you're killing me," I said.

"You have to. Otherwise mistakes start to happen and people start to get sick."

* * *

After two more tasting stops, Heather had the wild idea of making a reservation at the second most expensive restaurant in Northern California. Cyrus in Healdsburg was being hailed as more delicious than The French Laundry in Yountville, with a rumored reservation policy of booking months in advance. Surprisingly, on a holiday weekend during harvest, they had room for a party of two on the early side. When I had a free moment, I dialed the automated line to my bank to ensure I had enough for this cavalier move. If I brought wine and paid corkage instead of ordering off the bottle list, I'd just barely make it out financially alive. I'd packed a bottle of Talley Rosemary's Vineyard Pinot for the day, so it was on.

We parked on North Street in downtown Healdsburg and walked in to announce our six o'clock reservation. The hostess at the podium looked us over and scowled at Heather's shorts.

"I'm sorry, but we have a dress code in the dining room."

Heather turned beet red. I thought it was silly since it was still hot outside.

"You can sit in the bar, but we don't allow shorts in the main dining room."

"Do you wanna just chill at the bar?" I asked her. "I really don't care." She was looking down and taking it more seriously than she should have. The hostess picked up on it and told us to wait as she checked with her manager. She returned and said that she could put us in a back corner in a half hour. We accepted and headed to the long, dark, wooden bar, where a young bartender with a prominent flavor-saver was clipping herbs for an elaborate cocktail.

The wine list he eventually handed me was gigantic, as expected, and, after freezing up over the sight of their by-the-glass wines and inflated prices, I spied a half bottle of Domaine Tempier Bandol Rosé and ordered it. We quaffed it at the bar and the cool, aromatic blush of grapefruit and roses cooled down any hard feelings of our near rejection. We were seated with our glasses a bit sooner than expected and the extravagance began. I'd never seen service like this before, nor upselling either. Before menus were even distributed, a guy wheeled out a cart stocked with caviar and Champagne and was nearly shoveling out grams of the stuff before I inquired about pricing. He provided a menu then and I passed on it in the nick of time. Heather was okay with it, saying she wasn't a fan of caviar, and we still had rosé in our glasses. That would have started the tab off at $400.

Dinner was everything a high-end dining experience should be. The service was presidential, the plates like artwork. I felt like I'd inhabited a different body for a day, sitting here with Heather and drinking and eating like royalty. We were in Cyrus for four hours, and she graciously offered to split the check with me at the end. It would have cost me a week's salary at Hirsch. I had a six a.m. start time ahead of me and it was nearly 11 p.m. with an hour-long drive back.

CHAPTER 23

The Chardonnay load came, appropriately enough, on Labor Day. Mick stormed in at 6:10 a.m. with a red, rattled face and jerky body language. I'd already turned on the lights and raised the shop room roll-up door. He barked at us all morning. Old Bertha, the wine press, had a lazy two-hour per ton press cycle, and there were six tons of Chardonnay clusters to press. David wanted to hand sort the Chardonnay grapes as well, and since they wouldn't be destemmed before going into the press, we had to awkwardly dismantle the upper sorting table, and then forklift it down below and set up an "L" with the second sorting table to bypass the destemmer. It was the first year that white wine would be processed on site, so some chaos was to be expected.

An article in *Wine and Spirits Magazine* praised a Chardonnay experiment Mick and David did, where the Chardonnay was pressed and fermented in glass carboys, and they bottled a hundred bottles of it non-commercially. The article mentioned how David showed up at a fine NYC restaurant in the late afternoon and invited the editor down to try a bottle of it, which spawned an entire story about the brilliance of unoaked Chardonnay. And because of this, David decided that we would be pressing Chardonnay out of Bertha into a premeditated combination of stainless steel tanks, French Oak barrels, and 14-gallon Italian glass carboys. As you can imagine, setting up and sanitizing each fragile vessel dragged the process out even longer, but it was interesting, and all in honor of David's quest of paying attention to the fruit from his land and what the vintage demanded.

I was sent out to collect grape samples, and when I returned and brought them into the lab and office to crush, I made the mistake of honestly answering

Mick's question, "So, where did you guys end up going yesterday?"

"Well," I began to answer him as he started checking the PH and acids of the first juice samples, "we started out with a tour of William Selyem, so I was able to meet Bob Cabral and check out the place." That one was met with silence, since Mick had recently told me that I probably could never get in to taste wine there.

"Were you able to taste the wines?"

"He poured us their Weir Vineyard Pinot from Yorkville Highlands."

"Okay." A long pause. "That's a nice wine."

"I met one of the interns there."

"They have a sea of people working there," Mick said with an intense look.

"Then we went to Lynmar and had a cool outdoor tasting. They serve it in flights. We drove to Bottle Barn after and I picked up some bottles. Have you ever bought wine there?"

"Oh yeah. Yes."

"That place is insane. The selection, the prices. I bought quite a bit."

"It bothers me that they don't have a case discount. Everywhere else does."

"Yeah, I know," I said. "So then we went crazy and had dinner at Cyrus."

That garnered the longest, hardest silence yet.

"That *is* crazy."

"I know. It was a three-and-a-half hour dinner. We got back to the ranch at, like, twelve-fifteen in the morning."

"They still have our wines on the list?"

"I saw only one vintage on there, for one hundred and twenty."

"Yeah."

"I have to say, it was the nicest restaurant that I've ever been to."

"Anne and I went and sat at the bar and had drinks and some things to nibble on, and we left there spending three-twenty five."

"Yeah, I was lucky I was there with a girl who doesn't mind going Dutch, but we still dropped two-hundred each."

After more silence, Mick said, "Well, my Sunday consisted of running to Home Depot, then to True Value, and then over to Ace Hardware."

"Oh man, don't tell me."

I thought we were joking, having a good chat. Then he gave me a hard stare.

"It was all for the winery. Things *we* needed."

It was back to silence. Maybe I should've downplayed such a monumental day off? Good thing I didn't add to the equation how she spent a good hour after dinner riding me like a thoroughbred at the Kentucky Derby.

David, on the other hand, was excited when I told him about Cyrus, and more so when I told him how the Sonoma Coast Pinot Noir portion of their wine list featured nine wines from his vineyard out of the 16 selections available.

"Hey Marie! Did you hear that?!" he shouted to her with pride. The 1996 Williams Selyem Hirsch that Heather and I had drunk on Bastille Day was chiming in at $265 on that list.

* * *

At lunch I ate a bowl of soup and listened to my voicemails from the weekend. My dad called to check in, as did my mother who had mailed up a snakebite kit from Wal-Mart the week before. Then I got the news that not only had Mary gotten the harvest position at Seaview, she had already moved up and was working. She had tried to call me a handful of times over Labor Day weekend. In a silly way, I felt like there were eyes on that side of the ridge, and that I'd been spotted with Heather on Fort Ross Road or something. I called her back and left her a congratulatory voicemail. I concluded by telling her that things were starting to get ugly on this side of the mountain and that I'd call again soon.

* * *

Something about the Chardonnay or the Cyrus thing set Mick off on a dark, bitchy tangent that had only gotten worse. He was withdrawn and acting like a pissed off robot, snapping at Barbara and I and wearing the same dirty cargo pants and t-shirt everyday. The moody culmination was Tuesday night's horrible Chardonnay split-shift, which was the first time it was only he and I working together. After starting work at six a.m., I was told to take a nap at four p.m. and return two hours later for the night shift. The old press was clearly not in a position to handle the amount of Chardonnay that was picked and stacked in the new barrel room. After the final pressing, Mick stood there with his arms crossed, watching me angrily struggle to wash every last grape seed out of old Bertha in the dark. He finally told me to stop. I threw the hose at the wall and cussed, and he just stood there analyzing me. I was soaked, trembling in anger, and doing everything I could to keep it together.

"See ya in a couple hours," he said as I stormed off. There would be no later start time on account of going excessively late. This wasn't how you treated a harvest intern. If I was his full-time assistant and training to become the main winemaker, sure; but you don't work a temporary cellar worker for ten hours straight, toss them a two hour "recovery" break, then bust their ass for another eight hour run, only to be thankless and give them the verbal jab of "See ya in a couple hours."

I was probably quitting after all. I was getting paid a flat rate of $500 a week with no overtime and had worked 160 hours in the last two weeks, equaling $6.25 an hour. Barbara's arrangement wasn't much better, and we were all ill-rested, cranky, and perilously close to an accident going down.

When he said that to my back on the way out, I knew it was late but didn't know what time it really was. Once I was inside my truck with the keys in the ignition, the electrical display came on reading "1:58 a.m." I cried and screamed "Fuck!" I called Mary back to leave her a message since it was so late, but she picked up.

"Oh no," she said, instead of "hello." She knew. She'd worked harvest at four different wineries and knew it wasn't right to work someone like that. Bob from Williams Selyem knew too.

Barbara and Mike had just pulled up in front of the winery at six a.m. when I insanely returned, looking like I'd been struck by lightning. Getting out of their truck, they were shocked to see me there.

"What're you doin' here?" she asked me, since she'd been allowed to go home at seven p.m. the night before.

I gave her a knowing look. "He told me six a.m."

"How late did you work till?"

"Two in the morning."

"Nah. That's not right."

Mike gave me a serious I'm-on-your-side look. God Bless these people. I hoofed it down the steps and that's when I heard Mick's footsteps coming from the opposite end of the crush pad. He probably heard us talking.

I felt as crazy as the early morning I found my ex-wife's car parked behind a shopping center by her lover's house in Arcata and had the realization that I had to leave her. That same awful hissing electricity was within me. I didn't acknowledge Mick at all and found myself getting the drums full of sodium percarbonate and citric acid ready for the day's work. In hindsight, I should have just showed up drunk. David arrived at 6:30 and got me, Mike, Barbara, and Mick together for a pow-wow.

"Now look," David said, "I know you guys are working hard and I want you to know I really appreciate it. This week is a—well, it's a wild week here, with the Chardonnay and these young vines. I've asked the guys to help clean up the crush pad today so you can try to get out of here by six or so. But I need you all to hang in there for these next three days so we can get all these young vines picked and processed." He looked at all of us for commentary. Mick was staring at me, waiting for me to say something about last night or snap, but I didn't. I had fantasies of doing so, like the one I had where I envisioned taking a heavy tank valve and lobbing it at his skull as he computed his little additions whilst sitting on his falafel-smelling ass in the storeroom. Three more days of this at that sleepless moment seemed like a violent, eternal ocean of grapes to swim through, and I was biting my tongue and diving right into its torrential flow.

* * *

At lunch, I ate lying down and called my bank to find out about my financial situation after that all-out weekend with Heather. I had $500 in there, with a check for two grand being deposited on Monday. Also, being the enological prodigal son I am, I put in a call to Rob in Oregon, who still hadn't hired anyone. I was going on three hours of sleep. Not even a vision of being a tasting room manager again and having a stretch limo pull up in front with a bunch of puka-shell necklace wearing frat boys getting out to wine taste with beers in their hands made me want to stay and rough this out. This job was total insanity. I prayed that I would compose myself professionally that afternoon.

I pulled back up to the winery as all the vineyard guys were coming off their break to go pull bird netting off of certain harvested blocks. I was blasting a song with the hook of "Everybody gonna die one day, whether it be natural causes or gun play" by Lloyd Banks of G-Unit. That's the song that was getting me up to the job site three mornings in a row. Barbara was there dealing with Bertha and the nightmare of how every other time you pressed "left" or "right" to spin the grape-loaded bladder cylinder, it lost power and you had to open up the electronic panel and push this blue fuse. She was still pressing the load that was starting to barely drizzle into the yellow drain pan when I'd left for lunch.

"Is this thing still goin'?" I asked her, disregarding my new bad habit of dropping the letter "g" while in her company.

In the terrifying midst of hundreds of yellow jackets and bees, we released the bladder pressure and started the cleanup duties, taking all the cast iron screens off Bertha, as well as the rods that locked them in place, and pumping the last bit of juice into the tank. I was the last person who'd want to be in the company of even one bee, and now Barbara and I had to enter the swarm of them to switch out the load and bring in a new one. It was absurd how many of them were swarming at that mid-day moment for a taste of Chardonnay. The colonial word was out. I'd read how a bee will fly up to three miles from their hive to find their sugar for the day, so these gourmand bees were probably traversing from Seaview to Hirsch. Not bad eateries, by any means. I remembered back in 2001 at Whitethorn winery when Tasha elected me to hose out a dozen empty, sticky bins in the sun. I must've looked like I was loaded on PCP and thrashing around to the soundtrack of hardcore techno with that hose in my hand, opening liquid fire on black wasps and yellow jackets.

The bees who partied in excess lined the drain pan in blissful, drunken purgatory. I had been stung twice already that week during the hand sort, and it was a miracle that I hadn't gotten bit yet doing the Chardonnay pressings. With the day's more populous cloud of them, I didn't see how we *couldn't* get stung.

During the changeover, Barbara quickly took a sting to the hand as she removed a rod.

"Dag gummit!" she shouted.

"You all right?"

"Yeah. He got me." She showed me the sting as her hand started swelling.

"Oh, man," I said with fear, tripping on the red, animated skin of her palm. "Yours swells way more than mine." She held it under the outside faucet for a couple minutes, then came right back out to help me.

"Are you sure you're ready?" I said, hosing off the press as it spun around, loosening up the pressed clusters inside. The bees were going nuts in the sugary mist.

"Yeah, I'm good," she said. She was a trooper. But within two minutes she wailed again. A second sting. Back to back.

I walked over to the hand sorting line where Mick, David, and the crew were processing more of the young vine Pinot.

"Barbara just took back to back stings!" I yelled to Mick.

He had an alarmed look on his face, with his severe allergy at the forefront.

"I'll be right down," he said, running down to help. He took Barbara into the storeroom to give her some Benadryl. I put on the heavy gloves we used to fill the propane tank and prepared for all out Anthophilian warfare. It was time to duck into the swarm and pull out the heavy press pan and rinse it out.

Kneeling down with the suckers buzzing in my ear, I took a deep breath through my nostrils and batted away at a few of them. I reached up and under the iron lip of the press pan to pull the heavy beast out from under the press. Suddenly, a wild sting electrocuted my right index fingertip and beyond. I saw a flash of white. I may have shrieked. It was like sticking your finger into a light socket, or touching some comical electric gag buzzer which sent me into an allergic, heart-pounding reaction, complete with body twitches, swelling, and hellish hallucinations. Mick had just made it back up to the upper sorting table, and I silently stumbled into the storeroom to grab Barbara's blue ice pack out of her cooler. I fell into the folding chair with the cold plastic against my huge fingertip with a chunk bitten out of it. There wasn't a stinger, and I tried pinching the bite to eradicate any poison (which I'd just learned), but that only accelerated the pain. These yellow jackets were mean. Barbara came out of the cellar on her way back out and saw me sitting there, dazed, with the blue ice.

"Oh man, now you?"

"This one is different. I think it was a yellow jacket."

She took a motherly initiative and got me Benadryl.

"You just stay put, I'll go out there and switch the loads."

"But you got stung twice in five minutes," I warned her.

Soon David came walking by and saw the abandoned press and then saw me sitting in there with Barbara helping me.

"Hey Darren, you're not lookin' so good. What happened?"

"I just took my third sting in one week. And this one was bad."

David looked guilty about that and got right on the phone. He called Marie down at the house and told her what happened. Then he looked at us and said, "When this damn Chardonnay comes out you guys won't even want to drink it!"

Five minutes later, Marie came up with some homeopathic creams and I rubbed some on my finger, but this pain was going to last no matter what. I was nearly passing out, staring at the patterns on the floor and table as they moved.

Poor Barbara covered for me and started shoveling out that doomed press full of Chardonnay skins and stems. I sat in the room, sweating and shaking, when Mick came over and asked me how my sting was doing.

"It freakin' hurts far worse than the other two bee stings."

"Well, the hurting you can't do anything about," he mentioned in a loud, callous tone.

Then we heard shrieking out there. Barbara was standing up on the press, waving her arms around her face and head and coughing and spitting. We watched as she leaped back off the press onto the crush pad and managed to cough out a honeybee without getting stung.

"One flew in my mouth!" she wailed. "Eww!"

"What? Barbara, are you all right?" David asked.

"It didn't sting me!" She coughed and spit some more.

"This week is fucked," I said with my hand across my forehead.

CHAPTER 24

On Friday, September 7th, we finished pressing the last of the Chardonnay. The war was over. The final bins had sat around for so long in the cold room that a trippy, sea spray-smelling glaze had developed on the clusters. I think it was mold or mildew, but didn't really care. Barbara and I wanted to push big Bertha off the ridge or set her on fire. From Tuesday to Friday, we rustled and burned in pure white wine hell. David was referring to it as "that damned Chardonnay," and Barbara and I probably *would* never drink it for the bad memory of making it stung us to the core.

Emotions were all across the board, from the good morning vibes of the Furlong family to the angry energy of red-faced Jersey boy, to jazzy David who'd taken up smoking cigarettes and unloading bins of block five Pinot Noir. It was all there.

Turned out it was David's birthday. He didn't tell anybody and worked his ass off as usual. I only found out when I took him up on his offer of letting me use their laundry facilities. My jeans and t-shirt were going on day five and must've looked like I'd either been skinning animals or been tied to the back bumper of a pickup and dragged facedown through a Louisiana bayou.

"Say Darren, you can use our washer and dryer, you know," he said to me when I was in the storeroom grabbing some clamps and gaskets for a tank.

"What gave you that idea?" I joked back to him. With grape crust, bloodstains, grease, dirt, sperm and filth upon me, it'd take more than citric acid to get these rags back to a state of public decency.

With over a dozen actively fermenting red wine tanks going, I was assigned the sole role of doing punch-downs. Twice a day, I'd take the five-foot long stainless steel rod with a circular disc welded at the base, grab a ladder, and go to each tank, climb up, and break apart the hard cap of grape skins by pushing them to the bottom. This is a necessary cellar task during fermentation, since CO_2 bubbles up all the skins to the surface, leaving only juice at the bottom of the tank. If a winery is lazy with doing punch-downs or, with heartier red wine varieties, pump-overs (where the juice is pumped from the bottom of the tank up over the cap at the top), the cap can dry up, hit high temperatures and kill off the yeast population, or worse, form levels of volatile acidity. Mixing it all together two to three times a day keeps temperatures consistent and ensures that the juice gets significant contact with the skins for color, flavor, and tannin.

After I rushed through the evening round of punch-downs, we were released from work before sunset. Barbara and I were so elated we were nearly hopscotching our way to our vehicles hand-in-hand. It felt like a half day, even though we'd put in 13 hours. I used to complain about working two jobs sometimes and having no free time; here we felt like we were being rewarded by getting off in the dwindling daylight. I got home and happily stripped down, my jeans nearly cracking into pieces as they hit the floor. After showering, I picked up a wretched, fermenting trash bag full of two weeks of my soiled work clothing, which smelled like rotting broccoli and moldy dish rags, and dialed up David on my cell. He picked up.

"This is David."

"David, it's Darren."

A pause.

"Hello?" he asked again.

"David, it's Darren." Total confusion on the other end, so I tweaked the pronunciation of my name to match the way he would say it à la New York City. "It's Darr-in, right next door!"

"Daniel?"

"No, *Darr*-in."

"Oh *Darr*-in! Oh, I'm expecting a call from Daniel – my brother Daniel. Darr-in!"

"Hey, is now an okay time to do a load of laundry? Or should I wait?" It was a valid question worth asking via phone and not at his doorstep, especially since Luke told me his dad usually rolls around the house naked.

"No, come on over! We might force you to have a terrible glass of Spanish wine." He followed it with a laugh. "It's quite good, actually."

I grabbed what was left of the Tavel Rosé out of the refrigerator, but wisely decided against that and grabbed a Whitethorn Hyde Vineyard Pinot Noir. I uncorked it in my cottage, poured a massive Riedel full and covered it with the menu from Cyrus that you get at the end of your meal in an envelope printed on Cyrus letterhead (with a detailed account of everything you consumed). To avoid the polite confusion of bringing an unopened bottle of wine to a dinner party and having the host quietly stammer over whether they'll stash it or crack it, I'd learned this was the way to expedite things. There was a girl I knew who stashed every bottle I ever brought over to her house in her collection instead of drinking it like I'd planned. Even Trevor and Nate were becoming notorious for it.

I walked down to their place and knocked on the sliding glass door. From the porch I got a glimpse of David dressed up on the couch with a glass of wine, looking like F. Scott Fitzgerald at a dinner party. He heard my second knock and strutted over to let me in.

"Hey, David," I said with my bag of clothes, detergent, and the Whitethorn bottle. "I hear this is the best laundromat in town."

He motioned toward the washer and dryer in the back room. "You know how to operate that in there?" he asked me.

"Yeah, no problem."

He walked me over to the machines anyway and gave me a demo, turning on the switches and letting the water fill. I added in my bag of clothes and he sprinkled some of his own laundry detergent in.

"I didn't know whether to wash 'em or burn 'em," I said, closing the top of the washing machine. He started walking back toward the living room and I followed him in with the bottle. Marie was in the kitchen in a black dress with cool, silver dangly earrings on, cooking. She smiled when she saw me.

"Hi Marie," I said, walking in with the bottle. "You guys are all dressed up."

"Yeah, it's David's birthday."

"Really? No way. Happy birthday." I said to him. The table was all set. Some new-age tribal instrumentals were playing on the speakers. David grabbed me a glass and poured that Spanish wine he mentioned, which was none other than the 1997 L'Ermita from Alvaro Palacios. I'd read about this wine from Priorat, a massive blend of Garnacha and Tempranillo.

"This is supposed to be amazing," I said to David.

"It's fantastic."

"I brought you this," I said, showing him the Whitethorn. David grabbed the bottle and eyed the label.

"What is it?" Marie asked.

"It's Tasha's," he said. "Great! I don't have this one. Thanks." It impressed me how they dressed up and turned their country home into a fine dining house to celebrate. I got the drift that the last person David wanted in his face on his birthday after a wild week of harvest work was yours truly, but we sat across from each other in the living room talking about the wine. It was black as night and had a wild scent full of pencil lead, espresso, raspberries, and tar. I took a sip, and the powerful, gravelly finish lasted for a minute. David mentioned that they'd been to Priorat and met Alvaro Palacios.

"This thing could easily go another ten years," I guessed.

"It'll go another twenty or thirty," David countered. "It'll outlive me."

"You are welcome to stay for dinner," Marie offered. It sounded good, but I looked over at David, who was studying me and my forthcoming response. The restaurant business really taught me how to read people, and I appropriately declined. I thanked them for the laundry service and the glass and walked back up to my cottage with my L'Ermita to take the edge off that yellow jacket bite.

Mary came over around nine p.m. when I was folding my clothes out of the Hirsch's dryer. I was high, edgy, and batty when she got there. I apologized and we got down to it—frozen pizza, bean dip, cheese plate, and homemade wines. I was glad to have company. Washing the sheets just in the knick of time for her arrival did make me feel somewhat scandalous, but everything seemed lawless out here. We ate by candlelight, listening to a new mix of music I'd burned from David, and it was the second most happening bistro in the zip code. I was about to get a mere five hours of sleep again—a concurrent theme running since the weekend before. I was seriously deprived of dreamtime but blessed by the bounty of female company.

* * *

To be fair to Barbara and her love of country music, the next morning we listened to a Nascar-themed country music program on the radio. To tell you where my head was at, I was starting to like that song that went, "I ain't as good as I once was, but I'm as good once as I ever was." I asked Barbara who sang it and she said, "Toby Keith." The sound of roaring racecar engines and chaw-coated commentary by the top drivers provided a surreal overlay to the contemporary country hits. Mick and I even exchanged some laughter about it.

Around three o'clock, with David's prediction of an early end time giving us the frailest of hopes, I helped Barbara cut some green cheesecloth mats for fruit-fly defense on the tops of the remaining free tanks. We started guessing what time we'd really be done with all the destemming going on that day (20 -some tons of Pinot, mainly from the six acre-sized block 11, which was all clone 777). Fantasizing our end time was practically becoming a gambling addiction. It was very stimulating conversation up on the ridge. She was thinking we'd be getting off in the dark.

"I can almost smell the bacon sizzling in my skillet at sunset," I joked, cracking her up. I'd confessed my bacon fetish to her and Mick. I'd found that it was the easiest meat to keep fresh through a week out here. The lunchtime turkey club sandwiches had been top notch, and the bacon-infused refried bean dip after work had me reaching for rosé. Mick joked and said they'd find my body 200 years from now, completely preserved by nitrates.

Actually off at sunset and back in the cottage, I was stoned and using my boxers as an oven mitt to pull out a mightily doctored up frozen pizza. Drinking the rest of the two bottles of homemade wine I opened with Mary the night before, I ate and decided to write in my journal. So much had happened since the last entry that I'd need a week to truly bring my Hirsch history up to speed. It pained me to use a pen, since there were now 20 actively fermenting tanks to punch-down in varying capacities of 300 gallons to 1500 gallons. Getting up on those big tanks was terrifying, especially since I was foolishly working in a pair of old Doc Martens. I thought I'd fall off and paralyze myself for sure, especially in that state of exhaustion and with no catwalk system in place behind them.

* * *

With a thick, ghostly fog surrounding the cottage around five the next morning (my alleged single day off) and with the hands of a 90-year-old arthritic jazz pianist courtesy of the punch-down wand, I awoke and heard the grim reaper in his cryptic tractor, jangling and creaking down the hill, coming to take me home. "No fuckin' way," I said. Thankfully, that tractor was headed down to the Hellenthal Vineyard for picking, and I was graced with 24 hours of mercy.

CHAPTER 25

Barbara was sick and going on three days of it. Half the vineyard crew was sick too, no doubt due to the unreal exhaustion of the last week. How I still had my health mystified me. Blame it on the bacon.

For lunch I ate a grilled tomato, onion and cheese sandwich with hands that smelled of diesel. Mick warned me that we had a long, frustrating afternoon ahead of us, but that work shouldn't last past nightfall. He seemed a bit more stressed than the day before, which was surprising since it was a relatively mellow no-picking day. We had some tanks of Pinot Noir that had fermented to dryness and were ready to be pressed off their skins and put into barrels the next day. We needed to check the pressure of all the older barrels to make sure they didn't leak before we filled them. This required forklifting out a row of barrels on steel racks and blasting inside each barrel with the pressure washer gun at extremely hot temperatures, sealing the bunghole with a bung, then pulling out the bung slowly to listen to a particular sucking sound which told you if the barrel was holding pressure or not. If there wasn't a sound, we would fill the barrel up with water and put a bung in to let it sit overnight and "soak up."

I was now punching down 24 tanks and a one-ton bin twice a day with my Horace Silver-style hands. I was dropping weight and building muscle. It took me five hours for the morning round, thanks to the big, sugary tanks that were at the beginning of their cycle and had just been fed with the yeast stimulating nutrient Fermaid-K. The morning punch-downs turned into a boxing match. I now called the heavy, stainless steel punch-down rod "Ali," because it had knocked me out as I dipped it into a one-ton bin at face level. Going without a ladder to elevate me, I stabbed into the stiff crust and the rod violently jerked to where the foot bar swung right around and cracked me on the bridge of the nose. Blood streamed down my face, my nose going numb. I sat down with a freezer pack on it in the office for ten minutes, then went right back out and finished the punch-downs. Mick was impressed, I think. Before it happened, I was supposed to go down to David's house to help him load out the recycling bins, but the self-affliction ruled that one out. Mick went down there on my behalf, and when David came back, he saw me up on some of the *tankitos* punching down with a red gash ripped out of my nose.

"Darren, take it easy!" he said. "We'll be having the harvest party here soon. Just hang in there."

With a seemingly free night at stake, and in tribute to my colleague's illness, I rushed home, showered, put on Al Green and started prepping a garlic-rich lasagna. With the ingredients on hand, I whipped up a blockbuster bacon and mushroom lasagna with pesto sauce, three cheeses, and caramelized onions and garlic, and drank a Domaine Arlaud Chambolle Musigny that I'd bought at Bottle Barn. It reminded me of Heather so I called her, and she vented about her day and her boss's inappropriate power tripping. She drank most of the way through a Mayo Zinfandel by the time we got off the phone two hours later.

My hands woke me up periodically at night. I'd never felt pain like that before. It was as if they were broken. I took some Vicodin and smoked to ease the pain. They continued to throb miserably as I turned the lights of the crush pad on at six a.m. I couldn't picture myself playing the guitar or writing much in such a condition.

* * *

We worked an actual half day, and it gave me some time to wash dishes, shave the scuz off my neck, make my bed and clean the cottage. Then I went in search of waves and found none. It felt strange not to be working, like I was slacking. Salmon Creek looked the best for surfing, but it was marginal. I almost went out just to get wet, but ended up at Brew café in Bodega, where I discovered my D-Link wireless card was broken, a result of an incident when my laptop fell off the bed in the middle of the night after I crashed out watching a movie. It was a miracle that the computer still worked.

The gouge out of my nose was catching my fellow customers' attention. It was suspect and would've red-flagged me to any cop or bartender. I was positive that the older ladies nearby mouthed the words "wife beater" to each other with a nod my way. Afterward, I went into the record shop in Sebastopol.

As I was browsing through the jazz CDs, an older guy holding a coffee cup started staring at me. I looked up at him as he was squinting his eyes from a few feet away and checking out my wound. He could've been homeless for all I knew, so I ignored him and started looking through the Art Blakey albums.

"Who did that to you, man?" his quivering voice said. Judging by his tone, he was assuming an injustice had occurred, and he was skeptically in my favor.

"Stainless steel," I said with a smile. "At work." He took a sip of his coffee with alarmed eyes and nodded.

"Where do you work?"

"Cazadero. At a winery."

He nodded and then turned around and walked out of the store.

I went back to Salmon Creek and decided that the little slow left breaking in front of the rock pile looked worthwhile. The crowd had cleared out and there was some new wind texture on the water. I suited up and, as I approached the tide line, two lifeguard trucks roared up on the scene. A boy almost drowned in the shorebreak, and a lifeguard was waving bystanders away. I rubbernecked because I wanted to get the "don't go out" heads up in case it was a great white shark situation, which I was fully expecting at this place. Attacks at Salmon Creek had occurred in the past.

Out in the water, I was surprised by what must've been a 60 degree ocean, the packs of jellyfish, and how much I'd let myself go in surfing. I could barely function. I did catch one wave where I connected through to the shorebreak in front of the rock and got a cover up, but other than that I was flailing.

Leisurely pulling back onto Highway One north, I snacked on a bear claw and took the sharp curves one handed. Then I noticed that a California Highway Patrol car was aggressively riding my tail. My pipe and lighter were stashed away and I wasn't stoned, so I figured I was fine. I continued on for a couple minutes before learning that I was wrong. Flashing lights. I pulled off awkwardly into a seaside residential tract, fumbling with the protocol of being pulled over since it'd been four years. The young macho cop approached my truck on foot with a hand on his gun and a surprising amount of distrust. When he got to the window and saw the gouge out of my nose, he took a hard look inside my truck and then puffed his chest out.

"Hey there," he said.

"Hi."

"Now the first thing I'm pulling you over for is that your truck is so dirty that I couldn't read your license plate. I mean, I had to get right up on ya to read it. And secondly, your wheels crossed the double yellow lines on the last curve. I mean, have you been drinking or something?"

"No, I haven't."

"I'd like to see your driver's license, registration, and proof of insurance."

He stood there throwing on the tough guy vibe. I moved my guitar out of the way so I could open the glove box. Fumbling through it for the items requested, I envisioned what the cop was seeing. A total pot grower. Here I was, a bearded guy in a hemp hat wearing shades and driving a vehicle dusted in Hirsch *terroir*, with a huge cooler in the back and a guitar in the cab next to me. The Band CDs, sleeping bag, and dirty sack of laundry next to me failed to paint a more civilized picture.

"Have you been drinking?" he asked me again.

"No, I haven't."

"Not at all?"

"No. I just got done surfing." I handed him the papers, which surprised him.

"Okay." He turned to walk away and then paused. "You're not on parole or probation, are you?" he barked at me.

"No," I said, shocked that I was being asked.

"Alright." He walked off to call it in. Then a backup unit pulled up behind us.

"Great," I said out loud. "Two of 'em now." People were checking out the scene, walking up and down the street full of vacation rentals.

Finally, after about ten nerve-wracking minutes, he came back. "Okay, I'm issuing you a citation for crossing the double yellow lines. You, you just can't do that. Be safer. That's what those lines are there for! And, do you live on a dirt road or something?"

"I live on a vineyard."

"Well take a wet towel and wipe off your license plate before you head into town next time." He handed me the ticket. "Have a nice day now."

"Welcome to Sonoma County," I thought to myself, driving off and wondering when I'd get a break up here.

CHAPTER 26

The crew had picked 98 percent of the vineyard by the time the wet weather hit the ranch in late September. Barrels were being filled with the raw pressed wine and forklifted into the new barrel room for the next stage of their life. The workdays were still 12 to 14 hours on average, but were more organized and seemed far more manageable. We'd found somewhat of a rhythm, with Mick inundated with both educating us and the monotonous amount of legal paperwork and analysis he had to do. Barbara and I were pretty proficient in draining and shoveling out sugar dry tanks, loading up the circular stainless steel basket with skins, and forklifting each load up into the press. The sheer insanity of the first two weeks of the month had simmered down.

When the Saturday of the Hirsch Harvest Party came around, we cleaned up the crush pad area and moved tanks around to allow plenty of room for the 50 expected Sonoma Coast attendees. Rain steadily came down. David assigned me my first offsite mission to get ice, toilet paper, and avocados in Guerneville. The thick, misty weather on Meyers Grade Road made it seem like I was making my final descent in an airplane. I kept it slow and drove as carefully as David had urged me to.

Once in Guerneville, I walked into a café where a hairy man in a flowery dress came at me with a kiss two steps inside the door. I was too confused to react, but he turned out to be an employee of the place. A glance around the room revealed a co-ed, alternative crowd. I awkwardly ordered a cappuccino from the same guy.

I drove to Safeway after a couple heavy, suggestive leers in my direction and some futile fumbling with my new wireless internet card. Running behind on time, I sped back to the estate with the supplies. The party was due to begin at five. I had this nightmarish vision of the vineyard crew all showing up to warm cans of beer. I pulled up to the winery and found some wood planks set up on five-gallon paint buckets for seating and a lone stereo playing mariachi music. No one seemed to be around. Then I noticed our local part-timer named Linda out there in a rain jacket quietly pulling her tank samples for Mick to analyze before the party.

"Hey, Linda!" I yelled out.

"Hi, Darren. Can you help me pull a Chardonnay sample here? I can't get a good siphon off this tank."

She stood up top on the ladder and dangled the end of the siphon hose into the tank while I waited below with the other end and her sample bottle.

"Okay, go," she said. I inhaled and got completely blasted by the CO2 and unexpected back throat splash. My lungs seemed weaker than usual. It felt like I was suffocating, even after downing water. She apologized a couple times and tried to engage me in conversation, but I felt like talking would only diminish my air supply and I'd pass out.

David pulled up and started unloading cases of wine and Tecate beer. He was dressed up for the occasion. I offered to help.

"Nah, I've got it now, Darren. Go home and change." I wasn't really going to change, but I took that as a signal to do just that. As I hopped in my truck David said, "I'm going to open up a lot of our clients' wines tonight. Older vintages—the ones these guys are telling me to drink up. Williams Selyem, Littorai, Kistler... I thought you'd like that."

I drove down to the cottage and passed Marie and the couple that came from Seattle for the weekend. Throwing on my one pair of dress shoes and a Kenneth Cole blazer, I was out the door and driving back to the party by five after.

Once I pulled up in view of the winery, I noticed a large band of vineyard workers lurking back around the fence of the converted barn. Their arms were crossed and they appeared more ready to report to work than a fiesta. The party had started, but they weren't going over there yet. I waved, flipped around, and parked facing the way I'd drive home. I welcomed the guys and asked them if they were ready for the party in Spanish. It was strange to see all these hardworking machines being so shy and nervous. This would be the first social occasion shared by all of us, so it was understandable.

"*Vámonos!*" I announced and they followed me past the row of tanks. As we packed up and rounded the corner to the party scene, we probably looked like a vicious gang turning up to jack the women and the wallets, with me as the ringleader.

David, Barbara, and Mike saw us and said hello. Barbara was talking to Linda by a soup warmer full of chili. The vineyard guys quickly formed a human wall, staying far away from the table full of wines that David was opening. There was a stack of Dixie cups next to all the bottles. He had me open up some 1998 Kistler Pinots and a 1997 Littorai. I kept noticing my coworkers' awkwardness, so I told them where the beer was. They smiled but didn't advance. I went back to opening bottles.

"David, I'm gonna hand these guys some beers."

"Yeah, do it. Break the ice a little."

I loaded up my arms with Tecate cans and started handing them out. The guys examined the beers and weren't too enthusiastic. I went for another load to evenly distribute the beers and ended up with a can in my hand. I cracked it first and some of the fellas followed suit.

"*Te gusta Tecate?*" I asked Rígo.

"*Es bueno.*"

"*Que prefierás? Tecate o Corona?*"

"Oh. Budweiser."

"Wait. Really?"

"Amigos," David announced to them, "*es una fiesta aquí. Comprende? Es una fiesta! Si? Bienvenidos.* Alright."

Everardo and his two sons showed up and an older local couple, as did the Hellenthals and Barbara's son Michael and his girlfriend. The couple from Seattle stood around talking to Linda. Some Northern European gypsy songs were coming from the stereo, but the guys weren't feeling it. "This is the music of my ancestors!" David exclaimed. People were eating chili and drinking awfully expensive wines out of Dixie cups. The 1998 Kistler and the 2005 Hirsch were the clear winners on the table. Julí took one for the team and moved on from Tecate to wine. I made the mistake of telling that very inebriated tractor operator (who'd started this harvest party in the morning light) just how much the Kistler would go for on a restaurant wine list. "No! Si? Si?!" He was alarmed and, thanks to drinking all day, seriously close to pissing his *pantalones*. His Dixie cup was loaded to the rim with that Kistler when he turned to find his friends. Smart man.

I'd mentioned the harvest party to Mary and that she was welcome to come across the ridge for it. We'd agreed that I'd get a feel for the scene first, to make sure that it wasn't like the previous year's fiasco where 12 very sex-hungry field workers lined up to dance with the mere three females in attendance. From what I could gather, this year's fest seemed mellow, so before I sat down to talk to Mick and Anne, I called up Mary and gave her the green light.

Anne presented Barbara and me with presents. Barbara opened hers and it was a framed photo that Anne took of her on the green forklift with a very unenthused expression on her face. Then I opened mine and it was a picture of me on my knees atop our biggest tank in a non-Osha approved position on the punch-down catwalk. My ass was practically hanging out of my jeans.

"Hey, in the wild, they would consider this presenting," I joked as the photo got passed around. Barbara and Mike laughed. Mick and I talked about the Corte Riva Merlot that they'd brought, and then a little while later, Mick pointed to his eyes and then to my left and said, "Heads up." Through the wall of men came Mary, her hair back in a ponytail and dressed modestly in a black winemaker's vest and jeans. I greeted her with a hug and introduced her around the table. I explained the Dixie cup situation and noted that the chili, and apparently the rest of the food, was already gone. To make up for it, I gave her my top picks off the wine table and urged her to get in on that '98 Kistler before it became more historic than it already was.

"So, how're things goin' at Seaview?" Barbara asked her.

"Good. We're only about halfway done."

"Darren talks about how you guys got a chef out there?"

Mary laughed, knowing where this was going. "Yeah," she said sheepishly.

"And massage therapists!" I joked, causing Mick and Anne to laugh.

"What?" Barbara laughed. "Geez. We got none a' that. We don't even have a microwave!"

Half of the vineyard guys had disappeared. Julí was still in top form, going over to different people and getting really emotional about god knows what. He targeted Mick next, and the language barrier—let alone Julí's slurring state—made for a show in itself. Linda got the dance floor going and started grooving with some of the guys. Barbara joined her. Mick, Mary and I hit the wine table again, and I tried some of the Pride Merlot they'd brought. A short, older vineyard guy was starting to get a little touchy-feely with Linda out there, and we laughed as she kept deflecting his hands, towering over him by a good foot and a half. He was on fire; on this out-of-place dance floor in the wilds of western Sonoma County, Linda was the only available woman and his one and only pursuit.

A half-hour later, Mary and I walked off and headed back to the cottage.

She left her truck at the winery and hopped into mine. When we walked through the front door, I realized I'd left the framed photo on the table.

"Oh no! They're going to think I didn't like it!" I told Mary, calling Mick immediately.

"Darren?" he said with concern. "Darren, are you all right?" He probably figured I'd drunkenly driven off the road or crashed. It was a caring, paternal side of him that I'd only seen emerge in regards to Cornelius.

"Oh, we're fine. We're okay. My photo though! The gift. I forgot it on the table."

"Okay. Okay."

"Can you put it in the storage room for me?"

"Sure. We're looking for it right now... Okay. Okay, got it."

"Hey, thanks again, Mick."

"Alright. Goodnight, Darren."

CHAPTER 27

On the heaviest day of draining and pressing (in which 22 barrels of wine would be filled with Pinot Noir), I succumbed to throwing Spinal Tap into the CD player. It was time. We've all been there. Mick hadn't heard it since the 1980's, and I could hear him laughing as he did his paperwork at the table. "Sex Farm," "Big Bottom," and all the hits got us through the final hour of the day in high spirits.

He was starting to take an interest in my musical selections, specifically my new find of Old Crow Medicine Show. I'd throw on a CD in the battered stereo that Barbara ran over with the forklift, and if he dug it, I'd see him go over and quietly start looking through the liner notes. Turns out Mick was a huge Gillian Welch fan, and her musical partner produced the Old Crow album. We were connecting on that level, and slowly earning mutual respect as individuals with lives outside of the estate. I borrowed some of Mick's CDs to burn and brought him back a burned copy of Old Crow as a gift. He was beaming when I gave it to him.

I washed down the press exquisitely well for a load of our best Pinot, which featured the oldest Swan clone vines on the property. Some of the field went to Littorai and Williams Selyem for top dollar, but we apparently kept the rest. While draining the little portable fermentation tank as it was suspended in the air by the forklift, with gravity pulling the free run wine into new barrels, Mick handed me a sample cup full of it. It tasted nice already, with some concentration and sour cherry flavors. Not alcoholic or overblown, but a tight, red-fruited Pinot right out of the gate. He was smiling and seemed proud about the wines we were making.

Rain was on the way again, and Mick mentioned that the Cabernet makers in Napa were nervous about it, since Cabernet mostly ripens a month later than Pinot Noir. Seaview still had most of their Chardonnay out on the vine, which showed just how much warmer the Hirsch site was compared to theirs. Most of Seaview's Vineyard faced northeast, whereas Hirsch was all exposed hilltop for the most part. There was still about a ton and a half of our Pinot left to pick from a virus-ridden block that was barely ripening. The fruit had been hovering at the same slightly unripe sugar levels for weeks. David was anxious to bring it in so he could rest easier at night with the knowledge that his entire farm had been harvested.

After work, I found that I could do far more damage to myself if I stayed inside my cottage than I would driving these dark, windy dirt roads. I popped my jaw out on the phone, scalded myself with 120-degree water in the claustrophobic shower, and then ripped the buzzing clippers right into my ballsack with blood splattering everywhere. I forced myself into bed with a salad after that one.

CHAPTER 28

After work on Friday, I showered, changed, and headed down to hang out at Trevor's. I picked him up at his place and we went to a bar to have a drink and some fries. Trevor was talking about his new girlfriend, who was a single mom and former heroin addict that he was allegedly in love with.

"She's down to move to Kauai with me, bro," he boasted. He'd pushed his move-out-of-his-parents'-place date back to June, instead of his previously claimed December, and quit his serving job. He was waiting for financial aid as well as a wine sales commission check. It was obvious that he was plenty irked about my new development with Leslie and reiterated how for two years he wined and dined her, but it only proved to be her leading him on. I confessed that she and I had potential plans that night. There was nothing positive exuding from him on the matter.

"Make sure when she sucks on it you ram it into the back of her throat," he mentioned with a clenched pint glass in hand.

* * *

That night I decided to take Leslie out to dinner. I wanted to go to the pizzeria/wine bar called Picco in Larkspur, which Trevor once pointed out to me with the descriptor of "epic." Of course, now that I wanted to take her there, he gave me four other pizza options in Petaluma, all with absolutely zero atmosphere, and made me drive by one of them to scout it out.

"I'm sure it's good, man," I said, evaluating the down-home look of the place with video games in the entry way, "but I'd like a little ambiance. I mean, this is attached to a hardware store."

He was chapped. "Whatever. Go to Picco. Just be prepared to open your wallet *and* open your ass."

I finally fished a decent suggestion out of him—a French restaurant a few blocks away from his parents' house. The place was within walking distance. The reservation was for 8:45. Leslie worked till eight and was going to meet me at Trevor's soon after. He was trying to get me anti-socially stoned beforehand, as his ex-Marine friend Charlie sat next to me on the couch. We were drinking through an array of leftover wines from a gathering the night before.

Leslie arrived closer to nine. Trevor tried to get us to consider going to see some war film with his new girlfriend and Charlie. I declined and told Leslie we had reservations. She sat next to me on the couch for a few and I condidered throwing an arm around her as she talked to Charlie. We headed out to the restaurant along a quiet residential street. I brought a wine I made the year before and shared a big glass of it with the older guy who served us, who waived the corkage and offered a pour of his current favorite on the list, a red blend called "The Prisoner."

We walked back to Trevor's more affectionately in the cold. There was a chance their trio was going to pass on the movie and just rent one so Trevor and Charlie could keep drinking, but the door was locked. We headed back to Leslie's; she smoked two cigarettes en route.

* * *

The next morning I found Trevor in his spare bedroom-slash-office, smoking the remains of a bong load.

"Whoa, you scared me," he said as I walked in. "I thought you were my mom." The fact that his mom hadn't caught him smoking marijuana was an exercise of pure maternal denial. He was cautious, curious and still hurt—wanting to know if Leslie and I had sex, but not. I just left it unanswered for the time being and asked him if he wanted to follow me out to surf Salmon Creek.

"You're over it. Get back late and roll to Ocean Beach with me and Pete," he advised. "It's gonna be good in the city. Salmon will be shithouse."

"I can't. I'm cat-sitting for Marie from tonight on, and I've gotta feed 'em and let 'em in by six." I left shortly after and drove back to Cazadero.

CHAPTER 29

The week was heavy with pressings. Nearly every tank had finished natural fermentation. Our rhythm was rocking and we were exceeding David's expectations. Once Barbara got the green light on a free, two-day weekend from Mick, I swiftly made plans to go to Santa Cruz to see Heather and surf. On Friday, between pressing off the last mammoth 1500-gallon tank of block seven Pinot Noir, I took lunch, showered, and packed. Barbara and I had our pressing routine down. I wasn't so afraid of forklifting the grape skin-loaded basket up onto that press anymore, nor running the cycles, which freed Mick up like never before to get his paperwork handled. This was exactly the kind of challenge I'd been lacking in my life and I was thriving.

The fact that I was existing without the Protonix pills made me wonder about the root of my whole stomach condition. I hadn't had a flare up or puked since July. The weight-gaining ways of full-time tasting room work was a lot like being in the restaurant industry, but with much less running around. You end up tasting wines all day, and it's easy to move on to having more wine with dinner after work. I'd been operating this way for four years in a town that reminded me of my ex-wife prior to leaving it all behind for the Sonoma Coast. As intense and low paying as this temporary gig happened to be, the healing was priceless. It was clear that home is where the heartburn is, and what I needed more than pills and endoscopies was to spread my wings and leave the past behind.

As more and more tanks were emptied, pressed, and cleaned, I started thinking about what my plans were after harvest. If I kept performing well, there was a possibility of being offered a salaried position here. David hinted at that earlier in the afternoon.

"You know, Darren," he said to me as I was lining up a dozen sanitized buckets beneath the valve on the loaded press, "you've really got this basket press all figured out. Say, you and I need to sit down together, open a really amazing bottle of wine and talk about the future." It inspired a great fantasy of killing off a bottle of Domaine de la Romanée-Conti on the back deck with him.

I kept thinking about Australia though. The down under wine harvest usually commenced in February, and it had always been a dream of mine to go and work it. Mary had worked in South Australia and made good money and was able to travel around comfortably. She'd given me a contact person there to email, so I planned on sending in a resume over the weekend. Perhaps I'd be in Barossa Valley when the heavy winter rains of Northern California set in.

Since the Hirsch philosophy was to be delicate with Pinot Noir in the winery, we were never allowed to use the air pump to move wine from one vessel to the next. Barbara and I had been hand-bucketing each load of pressed wine straight into barrel, five gallons at a time, which is not normal for a winery of this size. When David bought the basket press and had it delivered to the ranch, the welded base it was loaded onto wasn't constructed high enough for gravity to pull the wine from the press into the barrel with a hose. So between the arduous bucketing and the punch-downs, I'd lost 20 pounds in a month, and that was in spite of having bacon twice a day. Every morning I'd jump on the grape bin scale and weigh myself, and Barbara would just laugh. She had her son Michael jump on it one day, and they were shocked to see he'd *gained* 30 pounds.

"That thing's wrong," he argued. He'd just embarked on a great new romance, and with that comes the weight gain of dinners out during the courting phase. I'd been through that before, before puking balanced things out.

Once the last basket of the day was loaded and the press cycle was started, I asked Barbara if I could run down to my cottage to brew a cup of coffee and grab my stuff. I wanted to leave straight from the crush pad. She was fine with it, so I drove down. As I pulled up to my place, I saw David walking out of the cottage with screwdrivers in hand. He smiled when I got out of my truck and we talked about how he finally *sort of* fixed my door handle. He was smirking knowingly about something while talking to me, which he was known to do, but more than usual.

"Hey, David, I'm going to Santa Cruz this weekend, so you know, you don't have to leave the gate open."

"Oh, yeah? Oh we're here. Santa Cruz, huh?"

"Yeah."

"Well, have a good time. Weather's supposed to be beautiful, even here."

"Right on."

"You guys almost done up there?" he asked about the pressings.

"Yeah, we've got one more hour to go. We got ten and a half barrels off block seven."

"Ten and a half? That's a lot. That's great."

"Yeah. Mick was excited about it."

"I'll see ya," he said, strutting off.

I opened my newly tinkered-with door handle, marveled at its solidity as I twisted and pulled on it and it didn't come flying off, and stepped inside. My mind chose to take in what David must have seen while he was working on the handle. My bed was made, the dishes were clean, the trash was out, his Herbie Hancock CD case was on the desk, my blue cooler, guitar and opened duffle bag were on the floor right by the door for easy access, and prominently on the bag, in plain view, was my mason jar full of weed—right where he was surely kneeling down and working on that door for who knows how long. It would have been impossible for him not to have seen it.

CHAPTER 30

The winery crew appreciation dinner at Chez Hirsch was set for Tuesday night. That morning on the crush pad, David told Mick, "Let these guys off early 'cause there's gonna be corks popping down at the house!" I was excited. Barbara was too, but irritated by the two-hour gap between our end time and the start of the party, where she'd have to rush home, change, get Mike, and return. I simply went back home and made some guacamole (at Mick's suggestion of always having a "nibble" before going to David's for dinner because of the resultant heavy wine consumption), drank some coffee, then dressed up for dinner. I took a Protonix pill just to be safe and grabbed a sweet split of Tablas Creek *Vin de Paille* before walking the 20 yards over to the house.

David was out on the front porch talking to Mike and Barbara while he fired up his ceramic smoker. I greeted everyone and handed the bottle over to David right as Mick was walking down the steps behind us. David was excited about my contribution.

"You know, I almost pulled a dessert wine but didn't. This looks great. Thank you."

Mick was wearing a green polo shirt tucked into his work pants, and Barbara had done something to her mullet since we'd seen her last, but I'm still not sure what. She had on nice jeans and a Carhartt shirt. Mike was wearing glasses, jeans and a denim shirt. We followed David inside where Marie was cooking. There were flutes out on the table, plus a decanter of red wine and a bottle of Hirsch "M" Pinot. Through the windows, the sun had just dipped below the ridge between Hirsch and the sea, casting a golden glow inside the living room and kitchen space. We clustered around the refrigerator, and after the greetings and opening pleasantries had been said, an awkward silence made it clear that we didn't have a social rapport. I think it occurred to everybody that we all simply worked our asses off together and that was about it.

David opened the fridge and pulled out a magnum of sparkling wine—what later was revealed to be a magnum of 1989 vintage Champagne that David bought from the winemaker in person at some bar in San Francisco years ago.

"It's all Pinot," David said about the grapes used in it.

"Why's it white then?" Barbara asked. Mick explained how you can make a white wine out of Pinot if you merely press the grapes right at harvest, as opposed to fermenting the juice with the skins in contact.

"Say, Mick," David said, "what about making a sparkling wine next year from the ranch?" We all looked at Mick.

"Oh-ho-kay!" Mick replied, as if handling this harvest wasn't enough.

"Well, anyway," David said, handing us all full flutes of Champagne, "a toast for you guys pulling off a great harvest! It really went off without a hitch."

"*Salut!*" Mick added.

We clanked and drank. I asked Mike how their son's hunting trip went, and Barbara chatted with Marie as she cooked the side dishes. David went back outside to cook a whole chicken on the smoker. I followed Marie's lead and had about four pours of sparkling wine. Mick, Mike, and I small-talked and ate off the charcuterie plate until David came in and switched to Pinot.

"I've got oh-four in the decanter if you wanna switch to red," he announced.

"Oh-four? Great!" Mick said.

Bobés the cat came in and cozied up to Mick on the couch.

"Ooh, Cornelius is gonna be jealous," Barbara said. Mick did the smile and fast nod in agreement thing I'd picked up on him doing.

"Hey, Darren!" David called out to me from the record collection room. "Come on in here." I walked in and saw him pulling out the vinyl. "What was that jazz record we were talking about awhile back? Hank Mobley, right?"

"Oh, it was Hank Mobley with Coltrane, I think."

He pulled out a Mobley record, but it wasn't with Coltrane.

"You know, maybe it was Dolphy with Coltrane." Framed on the wall in that little nook was a portrait of Eric Dolphy, among other jazz artist portraits, and I'd noticed that David had a bunch of his records. "Huh. Anyway, let's put Mobley on." He hooked up his record player and amplifier and blared the bebop. "Pick out a few more albums to play," he said. I looked through the shelves and pulled out Muddy Waters, The Band, and The Carter Family after he left to check on the meat.

Mick and I killed off the rest of the neglected salami and cheese platter, and I switched from Champagne to the "M" Pinot. Just before we all sat at the table for dinner, I put on The Carter Family. David heard it from outside and was so ecstatic by that move that he shouted, "Darren! You've got taste!" Then he came in laughing and beaming with the chicken and I overheard him repeat that to Marie, who was not amused by my mealtime musical selection.

"I'm tellin' ya," he said to us, "if I put this record on around my family, I get stoned. Literally."

David told me where I should sit as he and Mike took the table heads. I sat across from Barbara with Marie to my right. We had a great spicy chicken and rice dish to enjoy.

Minutes into dinner, David looked at me and said, "So Darren, what are your plans? You know, after harvest here."

Everyone looked at me except for Mick.

"Australia is a possibility," I answered. I'd quickly gotten an email back from Torbreck in the Barossa Valley, and the assistant winemaker there mentioned that he would be sending me a vintage proposal.

"Australia?" Barbara said, surprised.

"Wow," Mike added.

"How long would you live there for?" Mick asked me.

"Just for their harvest, like February to June. Mary worked down there."

"Oh, just for their harvest," David said.

In an Australian accent, Mick said, "Gonna make some Shiraz, eh?"

I told them about Torbreck winery and how their flagship wine Run Rig has a $200 price tag.

"Why not New Zealand?" David asked. "I'd always wanted to go to the south island, especially with it being so close to Antarctica. I mean, can they make wines with any complexity in Australia?"

"Yeah. Barossa Valley gets hot, so lots of the wines are fruit bombs, but Torbreck and some others make some pretty amazing wines from old vines."

"Well, you'll have to tell us all about it when you get back," David said.

The conversation turned to hunting and the large wild boar that had been spotted down by the Bohan property. I'd seen it on Monday night, all big and black with mottled white spots. It galloped alongside my truck for a short burst, then disappeared into the darkness.

"I broadsided one on Meyers Grade Road during the first month I was here," I said.

"Really?" David asked.

"You actually hit one?" Mike asked.

"I've never heard of anyone hitting one before," David said. "That's amazing."

After dinner we tasted the dessert wine I'd brought, which was a huge hit at the table until David started yawning and rubbing his face. Mike, Barbara, and David started talking about the old prison labor camp out here and how an escapee in the 1980's woke up an alcoholic neighbor in the middle of the night by gunpoint and had the old man drive him to San Francisco. With such a saucy crime story being passed around, I thought we'd keep the local lore going, but David was done.

"Well this has been great," he said. "Thank you all for comin'." Silence followed, and Mick knowingly pushed himself up from the table. We followed suit and said good night.

CHAPTER 31

My childhood friend Willie showed up at the vineyard on a rainy Friday afternoon. He was en route to visit some friends in Mendocino and I'd invited him up for a day, which would hopefully give me someone to surf with. Barbara and I'd had a pretty easy half day checking bungs and wiping down any wine leaks on the barrels, battling thousands of fruit flies in the process. Their population in the cellar had blossomed into a disgusting congregation, nearly requiring eye goggles and masks on our part when working in both of the barrel rooms. Any barrel that had wine seeping out of a crack or around the bung would be infested by flies in the morning, so we'd mix up a bucket of sodium percarbonate and scrub them off the best we could. My new goal for the rest of the year was not to inhale one, and so far I'd been achieving it.

Willie had a longer than expected drive out to the vineyard, especially with the low cloud cover. I met him at the winery, then he followed me down to the cottage. We were hoping to get a surf in, then he was going to spend the night before continuing on his way to Mendocino. David and Marie were inside their house with a fire going, spending the rest of the day in leisure. I'd rolled two joints the night before in anticipation of Willie's arrival, so once inside, I loaded up a French press of organic dark roast coffee, turned on some jazz, and we caught up over a cloud of smoke. Normally, I'd crack a window in my little living space, but with the rain coming down so steadily, we simply hotboxed the room. We were laughing at our position, sitting there in such a thick fog of our own creation by the time the joint was almost done.

Out of nowhere, we heard footsteps on the front porch.

"Hey Darren!" David called out, knocking on the door. I looked at Willie in fear, and he returned the expression. He was sacked from his last job as a camp counselor for getting caught smoking weed in his trailer after work, and now he was seeing it happen to me. There was a knowing, time-to-face-the-music look of empathy all over his face.

"Oh man, should I answer it?" I whispered, totally high. The truth was, my truck and Willie's car were out front, there was no way I'd be asleep by then, and the cottage wasn't big enough to lie later and say you were in some other room. I rose off the chair to pay the piper.

Opening the door, a blast of chronic smoke blew out onto David's face, mustache and hat, and he took a step back and gave me his signature smirk. "Whoa-ho Darren. How ya makin' out?" he asked me.

"Good. Good." I was expecting the ax at any second.

He was wearing a denim jacket and holding three bottles of wine. "Hey, I've got some wines for ya." I wasn't even hearing him. I was having an out of body experience as more smoke continued to drift onto my boss. I thought that maybe he'd say "Pack up, you're finished." But instead, he smiled and said, "Two of them might be last offs from the oh-five Estate, and the other one might be one of Everardo's wines. Be careful with that one. Ha!"

At that moment, I wondered if offering my boss a joint was the way to go. I wasn't being fired, but then I could've been perceived as a hold out. "Who's Subaru is that?" he asked, motioning towards Willie's car.

"Oh, my friend Willie came up on his way to Mendocino." I thought about introducing Willie, who was still out of view, but decided against it. "We're gonna try to surf in a bit."

David nodded, heard the jazz, got more of the marijuana stink, then smiled and said, "Well, have a great time. I'll see ya."

"Thanks for the wines, David," I said, trembling with the three bottles in my hands as he walked off.

I closed the door, set the wines down on the counter, then looked at Willie in silence. I was sober already.

"I probably shouldn't have opened the door."

"Nah. You had to."

"I know. Should I have introduced you?"

"No way. Not like that."

"Yeah."

"Sounded like he's cool with it."

"Man, we'll see."

We finished our coffee, then loaded up my surf stuff in Willie's car and drove down a very slick, secret road toward the coast.

* * *

On Monday morning when I stepped into the office for work, David was sitting at his computer with his glasses on. He looked up at me.

"Hey, David," I greeted him. I hadn't encountered the man since the front porch smoke out.

"Hey, good morning Darren. How're things goin'?"

"Good. Good," I replied.

"Hey listen, we're gonna be slowin' down here in a week or so. Everything sort of stops and shuts down for the next couple months. So I wanted to talk to you and see what you had planned."

I'd known this was coming, but didn't expect it so soon. It was incomprehensible how hard and long you got worked during harvest, and then that pace falls flat and you're back to having a life and, worse, not having a job. Wine production was so similar to the restaurant business with its closing time drop off and all that staff adrenaline still pumping. I could see how making wine for a living could turn you into an obsessive workaholic, if not an alcoholic.

In anticipation of this, I'd been talking to Rob throughout the weekend about working in southern Oregon, as well as learning Merle Haggard's epic factory layoff ballad "If We Make It Through December" on guitar. With harvest in the Rogue Valley still in progress, Rob had about five or six weeks of work for me if I wanted to drive up. It'd be really fun to spend time with him and learn his way of doing things, since my brief time working under him at Eberle had taught me a lot about wine production.

David awaited my response.

"Well, I've got a friend up in Oregon who's been talking to me about helping him finish up. He's offering to show me a lot of lab stuff that I need to learn. But I remember how you said you wanted to sit down with me and talk about some things."

"Oh right, right. I do want to sit down and have a quiet talk with ya here in the next couple days. Well, here's the deal. I had an idea. What would you think about coming here in December for a couple weeks? You know, there's not a lot to do. Essentially we'd give you half a month's pay to listen to music up here." He laughed. "But, you know, Barbara's taking time off. Mick's gonna take some days off. You'd check if bungs blow. If the power goes out, I'll show you how to turn on the generator. Make sure the cats are okay so they don't have to take the trip into town and back, which makes everyone's lives easier."

The idea of having the whole ranch and winery to myself caused me to salivate.

"I mean, December is quiet out here. You know. Quiet everywhere out on the coast. We've gotten some of those torrential downpours the last few Decembers. Anyhow, think it over. We'd need ya here December tenth if you're interested. And this way we'd get Barbara a couple weeks off."

Even though it read like the synopsis to Stephen King's *The Shining*, wherein Jack Nicholson's character becomes the caretaker of an empty, haunted, snowed-in resort, it was quite a proposition.

"All right, I'll let ya know."

"How was your weekend?" he asked.

"It was great. I finally found a great place to surf up near Point Arena." I kept it brief since I knew that surfing was of nearly zero interest to him.

"That's fantastic. Alright, Darren."

I met up with Barbara in the cellar for a day of topping up all the young vine barrels. In the time since we filled them from the press, each barrel had lost three to four inches of wine through settling and evaporation, leaving a vulnerable amount of headspace for oxygen. I jokingly told her my days were numbered, and she was concerned about what I was going to do for work. I mentioned the Oregon situation, and what David had just asked me to do in December.

"You'd come back here for that?" she said, surprised. "Sometimes the roads wash out."

We dodged the agitated mass of fruit flies as best as we could, siphoning wine from a barrel to our pitchers and then filling every barrel to the top. A short while later I heard her violently sneezing when she was at the top of the ladder.

"Ooh!" she shrieked. "One flew up my nose!"

CHAPTER 32

On Friday, I got a dinner invite from David, mainly as a courtesy for being the feline hospitality manager while he and Marie were out of town. He said 5:30 would be good, which, together with the offer from Mary to attend the Seaview Winery harvest luncheon, made for a complete ten-hour experience of wining and dining with the Grand Cru proprietors of the Sonoma Coast. All that hard work was being rewarded as harvest in this AVA of the California wine industry came to an end.

I arrived at Seaview at 1:30 and was greeted by John the General Manager. He warmly told me where Mary was and urged me to get a plate.

"I got my Hirsch wine club shipment today," he said.

"Really? What'd you get?"

"A Chard and some Pinot with a cat and snake on the label."

"The Bohan Dillon. Nice," I replied.

The spread that their harvest chef from Healdsburg prepared was amazing. Two long tables were set up, hosting the vineyard crew, winery staff, and the six interns from all around the globe. Servers worked the area between the tanks. I even got a blue harvest T-shirt.

To return the favor, I invited Mary to dinner at David and Marie's. "Should I bring a bottle of wine?" she asked.

"Only if it's dessert wine," I warned her. "He's pretty picky about California wines." We stopped off at the vacation house on Seaview Road that she and the winemaking team shared during harvest, and she grabbed her toothbrush, some clothes and a bottle of Late Harvest Sauvignon Blanc.

I told her on the drive over that I was being laid off in less than two weeks and most likely bailing to Oregon. She couldn't believe it and was quiet for awhile. Her pretty blue eyes were concerned.

"I've been offered full-time," she said.

"You're stoked. That's so cool."

"I don't know if I can live out here year-round."

"Yeah, but Neil commutes during the rest of the year, right?"

"Yeah."

"You could do that."

A true gentleman may have wanted to add something like *I'm going to miss you*, but it didn't even cross my mind to say that. We had never officiated this relationship, which to me was very much a friends-with-benefits situation, and an easy one for me since she wasn't seeing anyone else. I'd spent the night at her vacation home a few times since the Hirsch harvest party. I was portraying the non-committal man character with ease and didn't even stop to wonder if I was hurting a friend in the process.

We arrived at the cottage by five, which was enough time to play her "If We Make it Through December." The ballad of an unexpected layoff still made me laugh, but I don't think she really saw the same comedic value in it. She politely listened to me play it all the way through and gave me a bit of a skeptical look. She changed her clothes, put on some makeup, and combed her long hair down, then we walked over and rapped on the back slider.

David was still reading in the bathtub when Marie greeted us. She hugged Mary and told her she loved her earrings, which were silver with dangly, turquoise-colored beads. I handed Marie the late harvest bottle of wine and a Talley Chardonnay that I decided to contribute. After making some small talk with us, she went over and knocked on the bathroom door and eventually David came out to join us.

"Excuse me while I come back to life for a few minutes," he said with heavy lidded eyes and a mellow disposition. "When I get out of the tub sometimes, it's like I've emerged from the womb all over again."

"Would you like some wine?" Marie asked.

"Definitely," I confirmed.

"Good. You're in for a treat," David said, opening the refrigerator. "I have a wine here from Friuli." He found a corkscrew and paused mid-twist to tell us about Northern Italian wines and the time he'd spent there, citing David Lynch from the book *Vino Italiano*, the Dolomites and the Adriatic Sea.

"Sweetheart, open the wine," Marie finally yelped. Mary looked at Marie, and they laughed. He stuck his tongue out, realizing the ramble. As he ultimately opened the wine, he saw the bottles we'd brought and closely analyzed the labels.

"Look, what it comes down to is that there's no better wine—no other wine—to have with a cold cut than a white wine from Friuli." We sat at the dinner table and Marie put out plates of chopped figs, salami, a cheesecake of sorts, and some bread. While some avant-garde jazz played on the sound system, we talked about the fires in San Diego and their emissions, water being the natural resource that needs the most protection, Mary's time in Australia and at Seaview, and the Bohan Dillon Pinot.

Once the yellowtail tuna was served and the Friuli and most of the Bohan Dillon Pinot Noir were consumed, Marie made a comment about her Ayuverdic doctor in Santa Rosa.

David lit up and said, "I'll tell ya what. This gal, you show up, she feels your pulse, then she tells you 'life is uncertain and you're probably gonna die soon,' then you cut her a check for two hundred dollars and go to the Burger King down the street." I lost it, laughing along with David and Mary, but Marie was not amused.

We ate local salmon and drank the Talley Chardonnay alongside an older Nuits St. Georges Blanc, which had the heavy roasted popcorn kernel nose going, but a good rich mouthfeel and some acidity.

David picked up the bottle of Talley and examined the label. "You know, usually when someone brings over a Chardonnay for dinner, we're like 'oh great,'" he said with a roll of his eyes. "But this stuff's incredible!" There were a handful of wines from the central coast that I had in the cottage, but only Talley struck me as the kind of Burgundy-inspired winery that David would actually enjoy.

Once dinner was done, David looked at Marie and said, "Sweetheart, how about a bottle of dirty red wine? I'm thinking from the Loire or Madiran." She looked at him questionably, since it was after nine and she had to drive into town the next morning. The fact that it was that late and we were still partying with David was a rarity, which any winemaker who's dined at this house would attest. He normally passed out by eight.

"Any requests?" he asked, pushing up from the table.

"Do you collect any Bandol?" I asked.

"Bandol? Domaine Tempier?"

"Nice!" The rustic reds from this region in Provence are built on the Mourvédre grape and certainly qualify as dirty.

"I'll see what's down there."

He ambled out on the deck and down the stairs to the cellar. Marie went to the bathroom, and I ran up to my place and grabbed a lighter and a joint in case tonight was the night everybody must get stoned. Listening to the Harry Smith music collections on vinyl, I figured passing some weed around with that bottle of dirty French wine might complete the evening. I came back, peed, and found Mary and Marie at the dinner table in conversation. David reemerged with a 2001 Madiran from a winemaker who apparently divorced his wife after the 2002 vintage and disappeared from society.

"When I read that in the newsletter," David said, "I called Kermit Lynch and told him 'Send me all the cases you can! That is a great story!'"

The wine was reddish black and intense as expected, with a heavy herbal smell mixed with olives and coffee. Young and rustic as all hell, the thing tasted like it was aged in rock. Marie excused herself for the night and went to bed.

The song "Mystery Train" played on the record player and David got excited. "I tell ya what, this is one of the best songs of all time!"

We talked about the Jim Jarmusch film of the same name (which I'd seen when I was 19, mainly to check out my hero Joe Strummer of The Clash) and how offbeat it was. I'd heard a version of the song by The Band, but this old original was even cooler. We left after 10:30, which may have set an all-time, late night record for dinner with David Hirsch at the ranch.

CHAPTER 33

O n Wednesday, Barbara had to stay home to ejaculate bulls. The annual semen test was happening, electric anal prong and all, with a vet onsite. Mick pulled me aside the afternoon before and said to come in at eight so he could have some alone time with David. I got in around five after, and Mick was at his computer. He ran an aggravated hand through his hair when I walked past him and clarified his irritation by saying something about technical difficulties involved with installing the new printer.

"So, what's the plan today?" I asked. He motioned toward the barrel room, got up and led me through to his list of remaining tasks.

"Let's see. Ah! Insulating glycol lines!" He smacked me playfully on the arm and led me outside to show me the materials and the bare pipes that lined the wall of the crush pad. It was a nice enough morning to work outside on my own with music. An hour later, I even asked Mick if it was cool if I ran down to the cottage to brew a second cup. He later came out and said that he was going to lunch and that when he returned we'd barrel taste the previous vintage at David's request. This was the sort of workday I expected when I first moved up here, and it was such a bonus to have it now after weeks of flat-out physical labor. Guess I had to earn it first.

We ended up tasting wine from over 25 different barrels together, spitting most of it into a communal bucket. An hour in, I was scribbling pure nonsense under the guise of tasting notes in my notebook. Our palates waned at 5:30, and as I cleaned up the glasses in the office, Mick came over and started talking about how his in-laws were coming to stay at their house in Napa for five weeks. He asked me how I got on with my ex's parents back in the day. I gave him a brief explanation of her mom—who was born to be an actress before children and two divorces put an end to that—and when I was done, he started talking about his deceased father and then mentioned his mother as still being alive.

He stopped and said, "My mother has passed. Just, uh, just before bottling actually. I haven't even processed it." He looked away then, and the expression on his face grew somber. I'd had no idea. I finally saw Mick as a man, rather than a cold machine on a mission to make the most serious Pinot Noir on the planet. I actually hugged him and he slapped me on the back harder than he must have expected.

"I better let you go," I said. "Thanks for the barrel tasting."

He smiled and did the quick nod.

* * *

I drove up the following morning and was greeted by the sight of Barbara and Mick outside of the new barrel room tinkering with the Sulfur Dioxide canister. I greeted them and stood there checking out the hassle. Barbara told a quick story about the bull ejaculation day, and I jokingly asked if they poured Pinot for the bulls or put lingerie on the dummy female that was used in the process. Mick told me to go in and see David.

"Get in there before the concrete trucks steal him away," he advised me.

David was a madman, going from workaholic harvest mode to the construction of their new dream home on the property. The man never quit.

I went into the office as David was going through a few bills in front of his computer.

"Hey, David," I said.

"Morning, Darren." He smiled widely with his black-rimmed glasses on. "Just the man I wanted to see. Here, sit down and give me a minute."

I sat at the plastic round table in the center of the office and waited as he went through his bills. Finally, he cleared his throat and scooted over across from me. "So, how's it goin'?"

"Good."

"Look, I really want to thank you for sticking it out this harvest and doin' such a good job. I mean, we *all* want to thank you. Really, it was a smooth harvest. I mean, it was crazy there at the beginning, but it all worked out. And I know Barbara and Mick really appreciated havin' you here. But I want to ask you, what are your plans?"

"Well, I am going to head up to Oregon to work with my friend Rob. But I wanted to let you know that I decided I'll be back here in December like you asked, to watch the cats and stuff."

"Great! That's fantastic. Marie's gonna be thrilled." He scratched his head, still smiling. "Well, I wanted to ask you, what facet of this business do you see yourself being a part of? I mean, is it winemaking, is it sales..."

"You know, I, I could see myself doing both. I'd like to keep my hand in the production side of it, since I enjoy that, but I'm also really good at selling wine, and I like to travel."

"Well, we're envisioning a position here where you would help out during the harvest, but also be the one to go and pour at all of these tastings, like the distributor tastings in New York, L.A., or Seattle. We're looking to get into Nevada and Texas. All these markets. It'd be great to have you be the one going there and explaining the site. Because I really think that the way for us to communicate our site and what we're doin' out here is through the people in the wine shops and the sommeliers, as opposed to scores or tastings. I mean, these are the people that are passionate about wine and vineyard sites like ours. But we just don't have the time to get out there and do that."

This was exactly the type of position I was looking for.

"I mean, we're growing. We made six thousand cases this year, and once George Bohan's contract with KJ comes up here pretty soon, I'm looking to get my hands on some of that fruit to go into the Bohan Dillon. These young vines are already tasting so good that all of that will eventually go into the Estate wine. But using George's fruit, well, that's always what I'd envisioned for that wine. Even though the farming down at the Bohan's is a lot different than ours. I mean, sometimes I drive by it and it looks like a Yucatan jungle and you wonder when they'll pull a dead Mexican with pruning shears out of there! But Marie and I really enjoy having your spirit around the ranch, and after the spring, or after you go to the southern hemisphere or wherever you go, we want to talk to you about becoming a part of *your* future. We want to be a part of it."

I was so flattered by this that I started to tear up. I thanked him and shook his hand.

"So anyways, I'll tell Marie about December. When do you take off?"

"I think on Friday."

"Okay, well make sure to let us know how it's goin' up there."

* * *

It would be the last day I'd work with Mick and Barbara for the harvest. The show at Hirsch was over. The crazy, wild, insanity-driven ride was letting me off on my own. From racking and bottling, to destemming, fermenting and pressing, to ultimately barreling down every last drop of wine, the vintage was a wrap. Halloween was here, and I had been given a total of seven days off since the last week of August. I thought back on an email from my former boss; she had given me the advice that harvest winemaking was a lot like child birth, wherein you have no idea how you're going to get through the pain, stress, and discomfort while you're in its wrath, and then suddenly it's over and you realize just how abbreviated that time in your life actually was.

Barbara and I cleaned the hell out of the drains in the barrel rooms, scratching our knuckles and getting the concrete as clean as it could get. It was redundant but important, and one of the classic tasks assigned to any temporary cellarhand at the end of the season. My sense of time was skewed to where the six-hour workdays seemed like an eternity and my new bounty of free time a bore.

As I turned off the light in the barrel room, Mick came in to make sure I was going out the front and locking up. I told him I was. Then he paused, looked at me with an intense smile, and extended a hand.

"You should be proud of yourself, Darren," he said. "Seriously. This was the easiest harvest up here since I've been here. Between the three of us, we made six thousand cases of wine. That is amazing. It really is. Thank you."

We shook hands, and I pulled him in for a hug. He welcomed it sincerely.

"So keep in touch, and I understand David is having you back for a couple weeks while they're in the Czech Republic?"

"Yeah. From December tenth on."

"Okay, okay. Well, maybe Anne and I can have you come out to the house in Napa and we can do some tasting. It'd be a lot of fun."

"Thanks Mick. I know I didn't know a hell of a lot about the equipment and stuff when I came here, but I want to thank you. I learned a lot."

Some tears welled up in the man's eyes. I never believed it was possible.

"Talk soon. Well, talk in December." He walked out of the storeroom, got into his truck, and drove off down Bohan Dillon Road with Cornelius.

I saw Barbara out in front of the winery on my way out, locking the door behind me. "Well, I really enjoyed workin' with ya," she said, shielding her eyes from the sun with her hand. "If you weren't here I wouldn't have made it.

Really. I wouldn't have. You learnin' that press and doin' those punch-downs. As crazy as it was, we got through it."

"I feel the same way. If you and Mike weren't here, I would've bailed. Especially during Chardonnay week."

"Oh yeah! That dang Chardonnay week! We've gotta sell Bertha before I have to use her again next year." She paused and checked for her keys.

"But really, thank you," she said.

I gave her a big hug.

"Take care Barbara."

"Good luck up in Oregon," she said as I walked away.

CHAPTER 34

With a case of wine, an ounce of weed, a cooler full of overpriced groceries, and two bits of luggage, I crossed the Oregon stateline. I took the 199 out of Crescent City and began the windy, emerald, river-like ride into Oregon. Emerging from the magical, redwood forest of the coast, I reached Grants Pass, which looked topographically like Redding, or even Fresno for that matter. Every chain restaurant and big box store seemed to be here, with their horrible, towering signage flagging down drivers along the eternally busy Interstate 5. I called Rob when I noticed signs for the town of Rogue River, as planned. Once in Gold Hill, I saw his truck idling just to the side of the off ramp, and I followed him back to his house.

In the cold, darkening light, I hugged him hello and started loading in my things. It was a small house, not like my Hirsch cottage was massive or anything, but with a wife, a baby girl, two big cats, aquarium fish, and a boa constrictor, the joint was packed. I felt like an intruder with my cooler, bags and wine sprawled out on the kitchen floor by the fish tank. Rob had cooked chile verde and offered me some. I left half of my cold groceries in the cooler since the fridge was already maxed out. I'd be paying a small rent per week and living in a pink-themed baby room with a crib at the foot of the bed in the Rogue Valley of Oregon, in a town Rob said was full of old people and white trash.

Over chile verde, we drank some Rogue River Vineyards current releases and caught up about our respective harvest situations. He was wearing a t-shirt and navy blue sweatpants with athletic socks. The Viognier, Pinot Gris, and Syrah were made by the previous winemaker and finished and bottled by Rob when he took the position and moved up from Paso Robles. He was impressed that I roughed it out at Hirsch and got offered a position. He'd put on some weight since I'd seen him last, yet his wit was sharp as ever and he still had that big smile that made him hard not to like. His wife Katie had put their daughter down in bed just before I arrived and was attempting to use the internet on their old, virused computer while he and I sat on the couch tasting and talking. It was late before we knew it, and with work on the agenda the next day, we called it a night.

* * *

Rob knocked on the door around six a.m., singing me a deep toned *Good morning*. It was dark and freezing, even inside the house. I got up with some new job apprehension and brewed a French press, ate some cereal, and soon we were out in the chilly fog of the I-5. I couldn't believe wine grapes were still out there hanging on the vine in such conditions. We drove parallel to the train tracks and the Rogue River toward Rogue River Vineyards—a red-trimmed building that Rob told me was originally an old pear packing plant. We parked and stepped out into the icy haze.

Rob opened the winery's roll-up door to reveal two rows of closed-top stainless steel tanks and three one-ton bins full of fermenting red wine in the center of the cellar. As expected of Rob, the winery was anally clean. There was a lab and office to the left, and straight ahead in the back was the barrel room, which was much warmer than the ambient Oregon air. There was a second tank room next door by the outdoor crush pad.

My first assignment was punching down three bins of Malbec and a spicy, green peppercorn-smelling Petite Sirah that was from recently grafted vines in the field and picked at low sugar levels with mold on it.

"Let's see what you got, Mister Punch-down!" Rob laughed, handing me the steel punch-down wand.

After mixing the bins up and cleaning off the wand, I met the lab girl Jenni who reminded me of a shy teenager. Then I met Guy Wilson, the owner of Rogue River Vineyards, whose big boots, girth, blue denim jacket and jeans fit the bill. He shook my hand warmly and welcomed me to Rogue River.

"Rob's told me a lot about you. Glad to have you on board."

Almost immediately, I tasted Rob's Pinots and a tank of estate Syrah that was going to be sold on the bulk market to a winery up in the Willamette Valley. I washed a couple tanks Rob's way, which used a harsher caustic chemical that could melt your clothes and skin off, followed by a citric acid and SO2 cycle.

"I want enough in there to make me cough, goddamnit," Rob said to me, mixing up the first 60-gallon trashcan with the cold water, citric acid, and a large handful of S02. "Now breathe that in D! Cough with me. Hack! You see that? Cough with me, D!"

"I'll take your word for it," I said, coughing anyway.

Rob filled two large tanker trucks with his Pinot Gris for a winery up in Eugene. In addition to making 6,000 cases of wine for Rogue River, he had opened up the bulk market doors for his boss. They were now selling large amounts of wine by the gallon to other wineries, instead of the old, less lucrative way of selling grapes by the pound.

After lunch, Rob drove me around the property. It was amazing that anything could grow through such rock. There was barely any soil here. From the top of the vineyard there was an expansive view of the Rogue and I-5. The Rogue River Vineyard was four times the size of Hirsch, and Guy was growing almost every grape varietal out there, including Sangiovese and Grenache. There was a good amount of Pinot Noir, but the Rogue Valley growing region baked in the summer, making it better for farming bolder reds. Rogue River had Willamette Valley winery customers that leased out acres of the vineyard like at Hirsch.

We didn't crush any grapes or do any pressings on day one. Rob had been lonely here, doing everything himself or with the occasional help of some of the vineyard workers. He seemed happy that I was here, and kept referring to Guy simply as "Big Country."

* * *

The next morning was full of the kind of fog that "Big Country" said "clangs right to your bones." Guy was chatting with us in the winery, shaking from the effects of his plastic, insulated coffee mug. He wanted to talk and Rob simply wanted to get to work, so I spent a few minutes getting to know the big guy. "How long have you had the vineyard?" and "Does it snow here?" were my conversational starting points.

"Tell Guy how much your Chard and Pinots go for in Sonoma," Rob urged me as we drained a large tank to get ready to press.

"The Chard at Hirsch is forty-five and the Pinot's, I don't know, sixty?"

"Oh shit. Is that right?" Guy said, stuffing his big hands into his tight jean pockets.

Rob pressed off the three tons of Malbec that had loads of color and northern Rhone, peppery spice. I tried to help. Maybe I did. I punched those down for him in the morning along with one more punch-down on the Petite Sirah that Rob was losing faith in because the grapes didn't get ripe enough. I pumped the Petite out of the bin later in the afternoon, leaving behind all the unpressed black skins. Rob came over and tasted the ink, shouting "Deer food! Give it to the deer." He quickly hopped on the forklift himself, picked up the bin full of failed Petite Sirah and dumped it out in the field. I'd never seen anyone trash a barrel-and-a-half's worth of decent black wine before. He swore it was easier than doing the paper work to keep it around.

"It didn't get there, D. It didn't get there."

Working with Rob again was fun from the start, and he promised to show me the things I was supposed to learn at Hirsch. He said he would make me assistant winemaker material by the time December came around. I was just hoping I wasn't one of the many "dipshits" to which he kept referring.

"I just don't like people, Darren. That's it," he explained to me when we were talking about the winery events Rogue River holds at their place and their dependency on his knowledge of wine. "They oughta hire you to manage the tasting room," he said with a nod.

* * *

It was pouring in Oregon. The clouds blew in the day before, but it really started to come down on day two. Rob warned me on the drive in to work that if the forecast is for rain in Rogue River, then that means snow in nearby Ashland. He hooted and rubbed his hands together with a sinister smile. He knew I grew up on the beach and had never driven in snow or black ice conditions. I didn't even own any appropriate clothes for this weather.

"There's not another winemaker in the state of Oregon showing up to work at six-fifteen in the morning on a Saturday right now!" he said as we pulled up at the gate.

I started off with pumping over the large Cabernet and Merlot tanks. Pump-overs essentially did the same thing as a punch-down, but with the help of hoses, machinery and air. The set up required circulating caustic cleaner through the hoses and pump, followed by water, and then neutralizing with citric acid and Rob's heavy dosage of SO2. He had me spend 20 minutes pumping-over each tank.

Afterward, we barreled down a bin of wild, whole-cluster Pinot Noir that was more drinkable than the equally green, Joseph Swan Russian River Pinot I cracked the night before. Thus, we referred to the stemmy, weird, fermenting bin of Pinot as the "J. Swan." I filled barrels of it later in the day, then Rob showed me how to run both malolactic fermentation analysis and free sulfur levels in the lab. I never took high school chemistry, so I felt appropriately lame throughout the clinical process. Rob urged me to take notes and transcribe them into a Word document with the themes "How to Run Free Sulfur" and "How to Run ML's," and to translate everything he said into my own language.

Later in the morning, we received the last of the grapes for the year and the vineyard guys and Big Country all came around to fire up the big crusher/destemmer and get it done. The fruit was pretty haggard, with a lot of unripe, moldy berries passing by that I was trying to hand sort like a madman.

"Whoa, whoa D, this ain't Sonoma Coast," Rob intervened. "This is gonna be bulk wine. It all goes in. Just make your adds and don't pull out nothin'!" By adds, he meant the scoops of tartaric acid, sulfites, and French Oak powder that went into every crushed lot. I stood there scooping until the 50 pound sacks of each were done.

We worked till half past noon, then met up with Katie and their baby Dylan at a Mexican restaurant in Rogue River that served cocktails. Most of the shops in that little town off I-5 were closed simply because it was Saturday. There was only one other table of customers in the place at peak lunchtime. Maybe South Oregonians were homebodies.

Rob, Katie, and Dylan went to Costco in Medford after lunch, and I sought out the alleged "downtown" of Grants Pass. This was an old town that must have peaked in the mid 1900's. A lot of vacant storefronts and knick-knack shops were on the main drag, clearly left behind for the Interstate-side big box stores. I missed the Wi-Fi café on 6th Avenue by 20 minutes, and resorted to grabbing a drive-thru Styrofoam-cupped coffee at The Human Bean, shopping for groceries at Gooseberry, then attempting to access the signposted wireless internet of the rest area in Rogue River. Trying to connect to the server was a painfully slow nightmare, which ultimately never opened a web page. I drove in a circle around the place with a laptop over my crotch, hoping for a signal and cursing all the while. Finally, I floored it out of there to the winery to meet Rob at four as planned. The rain really started to hammer down. I parked alongside Rogue River's tasting room and waited for Rob. After a few minutes, I pulled out my guitar and played some songs inside my fogged up truck.

When Rob finally arrived, he had me thoroughly hose down the cellar floor and sanitize the tasting valves on all the tanks. I fussed with the leaking fermentation bungs on the barreled-down and active Pinot. There wasn't much to do and he was clearly being cool by giving me a couple extra hours of easy pay.

When I opened up my email account, I received the confirmation on the harvest job at Torbreck in Australia. The winemaker in charge congratulated me and told me that I should be there by the first week of March. Rob was happy for me.

"Run Rig baby," Rob said, citing Torbreck's most expensive wine. "They're gonna work your ass off down there man. I'm bein' easy on you. Those big tanks in Oz? Haha!"

Before we left, Rob was carrying the biggest, heaviest hose in the winery across the cellar floor and said to me, "Here's you in Melbourne! Get ready bro!"

CHAPTER 35

On Sunday morning, Rob, Katie, Dylan, and I went to a cool farm and restaurant on the northwest side of Grants Pass called Summer Jo's. I loved the place, which was a classic example of farm-to-table fare and hippies with good taste in food, plus the added bonus of a thoughtfully-stocked wine room. I couldn't believe it existed in what I'd seen of the redneck town.

As Rob and I walked into the little retail wine zone after a nice brunch, I told him how blown away I was by the diverse selection of wines and the fair prices.

"They're hippies bro," he said. "They're not out to rape anyone." He was holding his daughter while I rifled through the bottles. I called out gem after gem, then spied a 2000 Tablas Creek Esprit de Beaucastel Rouge that was the last of its kind and not priced.

"Get it man," Rob advised me. "This is the type of place that fucks up and doesn't know on the price." He kept passing these tenor sax-sounding farts while I was trying to pick out two more bottles. His wife came in as he let another one go, and I had to cover my nose from the lack of air circulation.

"God Rob!" Katie said, fanning away the air from her face. I held my breath and hurriedly picked out a 1999 St. Joseph, Penfolds 389 Cabernet-Shiraz, and the Tablas Creek. A woman with her grey hair tied back in a ponytail came in to see if we needed help. Rob looked a little busted, and, aromatically speaking, I was ashamed at what he had made of her wine room. I declined assistance and swiftly followed her out to the register by the entrance.

"Oh good, some wine purchases!" she exclaimed, as if people never bought wines from her shop. She checked for prices on the bottles and there were none. "Do you happen to know how much these are?" she asked me.

"No," I replied to the loaded question.

"Can you show them to me?" she asked, grabbing a guest check tablet and a pen.

"Definitely." Rob and I made eyes and I followed her back into the wine room. I pointed out the Frenchy and the Penfolds slot, then told her how the Tablas Creek was just sitting on the bottom shelf by itself, unmarked.

Back out at the register with Rob's entire family on curious standby, the woman typed in 11.11 twice and I thought I was already scoring. Then it got better. She rang the $24 St. Joseph in at $9, the Penfolds at a realistic $28, then the ground shaker—the $50 Esprit at $19. Rob flipped and said "I hate you" seconds out the door, but quickly added, "I'll give you forty bucks for that right now."

Once in Katie's SUV, I said, "But you can just drink half of it with me or pay forty to keep it. I'd say drinking it for free is the way to go."

"You bastard."

"That is my favorite wine shop on the planet," I said, looking through the bag at the vinous loot. Afterwards, I spent the afternoon in a shopping plaza in Medford. Being in such a small house with a three-piece family, I felt it was important to give them space while I was here. While writing in my journal at a coffee place and looking around, I realized that this is the kind of place where soldiers are raised. The local families looked cold, pale, and down, trudging through the plaza reluctantly in their flannels and sweatpants, even though the mall was probably the highlight of their day. The cold, grey skies and buzz of I-5 didn't add much soul to the situation.

Rob cooked an animally-rare ribeye for me later on, and I contributed with an onion, thyme, cheddar, potato mash. I opened the Penfolds Bin 389 and shared the wealth.

CHAPTER 36

To better immerse me into the Rogue Valley wine scene, Rob told me we were going to a wine event after work. It was an open house at Troon winery for winery employees only in the nearby, beautifully manicured, tourist-ready Applegate Valley.

"The owner's son drives a Porsche and wears $200 jeans," Rob told me on the drive over. I'd smoked before hitting the road and was assigned the backseat next to Dylan, who was facing the rear in her little seat. "Let me show you a trick, D," Rob said as I got into the backseat of the SUV next to her. He pulled out a porcupine puppet for me to use. "This is Dilly's best friend." He threw it on his hand and did a high-pitched singing show for her. "Picklehead's got a big ol' head," he sang. I laughed at it, wondering where the plot of the puppet was heading. She was mellow most of the ride out there, but at one point, I did have to put on an awkward puppet show to keep her from scowling, with very little dialogue to match all the flapping of the fabric.

Troon winery looked like a glowing French villa in Bordeaux, with multiple buildings surrounded by perfect rows of vines. We walked in to the sound of white jazz with trays of appetizers and open wine tasting available. Some stereotypes about tasting room attendants proved to be universal: the silver-haired, tan-faced Leslie Nielsen type at the reserve table and the crispy-permed older woman pouring white wines and wearing too much makeup and jewelry. Sure enough, there was the guy in $200 jeans, who was rumored to be with the young, sexy blonde that was pouring wines behind the center of the tasting bar. I eyeballed the sheet of current releases and saw that Troon made over a dozen different wines. Rob and Katie got caught up talking with people while I sampled my way through the highlights. Some of the wines were decent, but overpriced.

I was coerced into a tour of the facility with Big Country's wife and Jenni the lab girl from Rogue River. The assistant winemaker who led it was a blonde, lanky girl around my age who knew her stuff. They had the tops of some square, jacketed portable steel tanks removed and used those for fermentation vessels. We tried some barrel samples of Cabernet. Fruit flies were everywhere. We were asked out to dinner with the Rogue River crew and their new national sales director, but Rob had made plans for us to drive to a winery across the way that his friends were working for, so we had to decline. Big Country didn't seem to appreciate that.

* * *

It was close to five the next day at work when Rob said, "You need to see this, even though it'll cost us a half hour."

There were two big 4X4 trucks parked in front of the lit up storage barn next to the winery. Rain pounded down in frigid, explosive gobs. I followed Rob into the barn scene—two men in wildlife camo, teen twin boys, and big Guy were standing around a huge, custom-welded, black cage built to catch a cougar. These guys in camo were prepared to get out there in the rain with it. They were going to throw a live chicken or something inside and tie it up. There was a triggered, wooden board that would slam down guillotine style and trap whatever ventured in to eat the chicken. The men in camo were, interestingly enough, also our IT managers for the winery and had spent the earlier part of the day working on the network in the main office. Only in Oregon do the computer geeks go mountain lion hunting in camouflage at night.

"Catch that cougar and we'll drive this cage all loaded up through downtown Ashland!" one of the computer guys joked.

"Yeah! Then let it loose on all the hippies!" said the other. They all snickered, while all I could think about was how fortunate I was to be Caucasian at the time. Walking into that sinister scene in the barn as a dark-skinned man and I'd be thinking those half-drunk Americans were going to throw me in that cage for bait and take me deep into the brush.

We returned to work. I did a bung check throughout the winery and hosed off the floors. I was thinking about that cage and Rob's permanent job offer he'd hinted at earlier.

"So Darren, what are you really doing for January and February?" he asked me. As far as I knew, I was moving back to the Central Coast around

Christmas to manage my mom's restaurant with my brother as she underwent a long recovery from leaky bladder surgery. Then I was most likely going to Australia from March on. Maybe my new Hirsch-honed cellar skills were actually winning him over.

I tried to picture myself living around Gold Hill, Oregon, but couldn't see it. It was two-plus hours to the beach, for starters, and the mall and what I'd seen of Grants Pass would be stifling. Out of curiosity, I looked up rooms for rent in the Medford/Gold Hill/Ashland area on Craigslist, and lo and behold I found one posted by a girl that mentioned two 19-year-old females who were looking for a responsible tenant in West Medford. I asked Katie about that area of town and she likened it to South Oregon's Compton, but I was determined. Make wine and live with two 19-year-old girls? It mentioned that the candidate should be "420 friendly." I responded and got an email an hour later from the girl who owned the condo. Through a second round of emails, I learned that she had moved out of Medford, but her friend and tenant named Karen (who was "fun") would show me the room. She gave me Karen's number and told me to give her a call.

* * *

Rob's approval came well undone at the end of the day when I pumped over 200 gallons of Cabernet into his Merlot tank—blame the Super Silver Haze, the extended lunch, the conversation we were having while I was up on the catwalk with that hose coming out of the Cab tank and pumping into his Merlot tank. He realized what was happening from down below.

"Darren, shut that off!" I closed the valve and of course wine sprayed up out of the Venturi aeration valve.

"Remember! You start the pump-over—then open the Venturi. Close the Venturi, then stop the pump-over, then leave the Venturi open." It would be an accidental right bank Bordeaux-style blend of my own making, with probably 25 percent Cabernet Sauvignon now in the mix. Luckily, they were being fermented with the same yeast and pretty much at the same sugar level. The combination actually smelled and tasted pretty good, which saved me some hostility.

"You're lucky D. You're so lucky."

CHAPTER 37

I called Karen and made an appointment to see the West Medford room for rent. All week long my mind was flavored with erotic coed fantasies about this three-bedroom condo. Rob's mind was vicariously on the same page. I was thinking about thongs, drinking, smoking, being the sophisticated older winemaker who was compassionate about their young womanly plight. I was seeing a lot of nights of hanging out on the couch with wine, weed and guitars while the world froze around us. In short, I was out of my fucking mind.

On the Wednesday of the walkthrough, Rob got ambitious and pressed off two big tanks (the Merlot or, as we now called it, "Darren's Claret," thanks to my screw up, and the Cabernet). There was a lot of anticipation going around. Hell, Rob was singing the theme song to *Three's Company* for Chrissakes— "Come and knock on our door. We'll be waiting for you."

He was bringing up his own well-formulated fantasies about it. "You'll be a father figure; you've traveled the world and you surf, they'll think you're all cool." But later in the day, when he realized that if the girls actually were attractive and interested in me, and that I really *would* be moving here, he laid it down that the person he needed as an assistant winemaker would have to be able to add bentonite and sulfur on their own accord and needed to know when or when not to add Isinglass and how to sanitize the bottling line.

"I've got a stack of resumes that I need to go through from guys who can do that," he cautioned me while we drained the Cabernet tank through the sump. "These next two weeks man, they're your audition. If you can really kick ass, then maybe we can do something. But right now, all this shit I'm teaching you benefits you, not me. It adds an extra two hours to my day. I need to be teaching things to somebody who's going to be around."

"If these chicks are hot," I said, "I'll work the register in the fucking Gold Hill General Store."

* * *

After work, Rob surprised Katie and I by taking us to dinner at a Thai fusion wine bar in Medford called Bambu. I followed them there in my truck so I could make my 7:30 p.m. walk-through afterward. We had a rich, savory Panther Creek Shea Vineyard Pinot Noir and some lemongrass soup that fried my esophagus as nothing had in months. I wondered if my streak of no acid reflux was coming to an end. I'd been so lucky since August, and here I was feeling a bit of the familiar burn.

We finally clued Katie into the walk-through at dinner; she thought it was hilarious and couldn't believe I was actually going. Rob sent me off with a "Don't fail me" look in the parking lot, and I departed into the poverty-stricken depths of West Medford. Thanks to my main dish selection at Bambu, my mouth smelled like a Cuisinart that had just grinded garlic, cayenne peppers, and a possum together, so I stopped off at a mini mart on 99 that seemed shady from the get-go. A burly, flannelled older gal was on her own working the counter and a fat, red-faced skinhead with a confederate flag bandanna on was chewing her out when I walked in. It was obvious they knew each other or existed in the same social circle. Whatever argument they were having, she was sober and he was not, so he left shouting a bevy of inebriated accusations, which she calmly denied one and all.

I picked out a lighter, condoms, and some breath mints like a candidate for an episode of NBC's *To Catch a Predator*. I lined up behind another skinhead that had the NFL Raiders' Pirate tattooed on the back of his neck, along with some other prison style tats that I couldn't make out—nor was it wise to attempt to do so. He was on something heavy, either drunk, stoned, or else high on heroin. It took the guy five minutes to pick out his cigarettes and pay for his fountain drink and candy bars.

Back in my truck, I locked the doors and started the engine. Maybe West Medford was gnarlier than South Central. If the turnoff was anywhere near this convenience store, then I was out of here. It wasn't, so I followed the directions down a mostly Christmas-lighted residential street to the alleged "condo" on Village Drive. I parked by a two story, 1970's era apartment complex and heard the thumping bass of a little house party across the way. As I got out, I remembered Rob's advice to leave my wallet in my car, just in case the whole thing was an internet setup and I'd end up getting robbed. I stashed it under the seat and shut the door.

I heard footsteps and a scampering canine. The night I called Karen for directions and info on the place, she'd giggled and mentioned how her Shitsu gets into everything. From my vantage point, the person before me was an old, drunk woman in a leather jacket and heels, fumbling up a stairway toward the correct address with a long leash on her wild, miniature beast.

I followed in the darkness, seeing that she was approaching the right apartment number, and I felt appropriately creepy. As I made it to the steps I called out.

"Are you Karen?" The woman and her dog turned immediately as she gave me the affirmative. She had her key in the door.

"I'm Darren. I'm here to see the room."

The dog immediately charged down the stairs and began jumping and nipping at me, which I probably deserved.

"Oh, that's Sammy," Karen said. "She's my little terror." I even petted the crusty-faced thing before skeptically following her through the front door. This wasn't a good start.

I was met with a stagnant, cigarette smoke haze as I stepped into the shag-carpeted living room. There was a drunk, Santa Claus-looking man in red pajama pants chilling on the couch and watching *Wheel of Fortune*. He had an empty pink donut box beside him. I offered a smile, but he just stared at me absently. In the kitchen to my right, five more pink donut boxes littered the counter. The meaty dog stink rivaled the cigarettes for most dominant odor. In the yellow light of the room, I noticed Karen's aged and hardened face, buried by sweaty makeup.

"This is Cheyenne's dad" she said. St. Nick and I could've easily not shaken hands at that moment, but I did it anyway, feeling his puffy, sugar-glazed fingers on mine.

"Cheyenne will be home any minute," Karen said. "So, let me show you the room." I assumed Cheyenne was one of the two 19-year-old girls that allegedly lived here. Karen clarified by referring to Cheyenne as her daughter. I followed her through the living room, and she paused in front of the first bedroom.

"Now this is my room."

The false advertising sure made itself known there. I'd been fooled. There was a queen-sized bed in there, dirty clothes draped all over the place, an old school TV perched on top of a dresser, and a well-used ashtray by the massive alarm clock.

"Um, I pay a little more, so I have a bigger room," she said, gauging my response to that one. This Karen woman was in nice enough shape for her age, dressed younger than she probably should've been, in shiny skintight pants and a flashy jacket. She led me past a bathroom with long black hairs everywhere and a million plastic containers all over the shower.

"Here's Cheyenne's room," she said next to the closed door with stickers on it.

We walked down to the end of the tiny hall and came to the room for rent.

"And here's your room." It was a smoke-stained box with a mirrored closet and hairy orange carpet. No window at all. There was a stack of large plastic storage containers full of someone else's stuff in there.

"Cheyenne would love to meet you. I think she'll really like you. So… so you can hang out for a few until she comes home?" We were still standing in what Karen believed would be my future dwelling, and I was being as polite as I could be, standing on that squishy carpet. "And I don't know what Ariel put in the listing on the internet. Something about four-twenty?" She checked my reaction to that.

"The price of the room?" I played dumb and asked.

"No, no. Four-twenty. You know? Well, it's silly that she put that in the ad. I mean, she bought this condo from me, so she can do what she wants. It's just, you know, I wouldn't smoke that stuff in front of my daughter."

"Yeah," I said, neither claiming it nor putting it down. Maybe that old man out there was just stoned off his ass and grinding a dozen donuts to Pat and Vanna. That's one way to party. Karen had obviously been out having cocktails at some Godforsaken local watering hole before this appointment. Was he living rent free at this place on the sly?

I followed her back into the living room where Santa was smoking off that carton on the cluttered coffee table. Karen started to flirt while *Wheel of Fortune* hit a crescendo. My erotic fantasy was swiftly gut shot and bleeding its economically disenfranchised juices all over. I lied and told Karen that the head winemaker at my work still had to give me the final okay about the job before I committed to a January and February rental.

"Oh, I like wine. You want some wine, hon?"

"No no, I'm…" She opened up her fridge, which I didn't even want to know the interior contents of, and rifled around for a bottle. "Really, I'm alright. I'm cool."

"I like sweet wines. Sweeter wines."

I felt pressured to have a seat next to the dude, but I couldn't bring myself to settle in. So I remained standing, saying nothing, watching the TV, and wondering if I should just make a break for it.

"You gonna wait to meet Cheyenne?" Karen asked me. And it would've taken this Cheyenne character walking in and blazing a joint in a thong, high heels, body glitter, and pasties over an augmented rack for me to even consider moving into this broken scene by now.

I told Karen I'd let Ariel know what happened with my position and that I had to go. The outside chill took me in its arms as I hustled down the stairs to the street. That house party had grown louder across the way—some large women grooving in front of a television. I was back at Rob and Katie's by eight. The front door was locked, so I just rapped on it until Rob's face popped up in the window in the door, giving me a questionable up and down. He opened the door with an inquisitive look.

"Man, I was duped!" I elaborated in a rapid-fire monologue that had him and Katie dying with laughter. "Man I can't believe that fantasy occupied so much of my mind this week!"

"*Your* mind?" he came back at me. "That was all *I* could think about!"

CHAPTER 38

I waited for the ice to melt outside before leaving Gold Hill for a Thanksgiving weekend on the Humboldt County coast. I was off to work the Whitethorn Winery open house and see Heather, and looking forward to relaying some Hirsch harvest stories with Tasha and the South Humboldt crew.

It was in the low 30's the whole drive out on 199. I drove up to Brookings once I hit 101 and encountered a hectic Harris Beach—no one out, currents, a few uncertain, side waves cracking hard in the middle. It deceivingly looked like I could've had a good, challenging surf, but I opted to head south and see if Crescent City had anything more manageable to offer.

In Crescent City I pulled up at the jetty and saw that Crescent Beach was okay—definitely more blocked by the big swell that was wreaking havoc on Oregon. I saw a wetsuit and hood-wearing figure come around the break wall way outside, so I drove out and found a slightly hidden right hand wave called "Whaler Beach." It was what I imagined the outside of Port San Luis' break wall to be like on the right swell. Three guys were out there missing the best waves. I suited up and paddled around the sharky rock wall, then out into the breaking zone. On the shoulder of the right, a reef was sucking up nearly dry, and I'd seen these guys getting caught behind. There was only one guy out still when I made it outside, and he greeted me warmly enough. I surfed for about 40 minutes, finding the wave to be really mellow but fun.

Continuing on 101 South, I took the woodsy Newton B. Drury scenic alternative and practiced my bad new habit of playing the baritone ukulele while driving. I got to Trinidad and found the waves at Agate Beach too big and mixed up, Indian Beach too flat, Camel Rock surfable but empty because of the holiday, and the Eureka harbor mouth not being the monstrous lefthander that I imagined. I resorted to the lounge of Hotel Carter, changing into nicer clothes on the street. I brought my laptop in and sat by the fire on a big leather chair and proceeded to drain a bottle of 1999 Leasingham Classic Clare Shiraz (for a steal of $40 on their award-winning wine list) with some butternut squash soup and bread. A family of three checked in to the hotel and then came down and sat next to me. Their daughter was probably 12 years old and yawned and fidgeted while her parents sipped on the wine that the hotel provided complimentary for their guests. The man eyeballed my sediment heavy and nearly drained decanter of Australian wine and we started chatting. I poured him off a glass, then discovered that they lived in Medford. I told them about Rogue River Vineyards and my experience in Gold Hill, how I'd lived in Humboldt and worked for Whitethorn Winery but really lived on the Sonoma Coast. By that twist and turn of my life's story, they really had no idea what sort of man they were talking to. Truth be told, neither did I. I wisely took my time and had a double espresso before I made the drive to Mourad and Greta's house in Blue Lake.

* * *

I got a haircut in Arcata before the Whitethorn wine tasting the next day. Heather was en route from Santa Cruz to spend the holiday weekend with me. A wine-splashed Northern California outing in unchartered territory had her fueling up and making the eight-hour trek. I started realizing that she was a true keeper, full of affection and perks, and it was a shame that our relations would eventually come to an end, be it after the weekend or before I left for Australia. Woody Allen wrote that "Unfulfilled love is the most romantic," and I was seeing that first hand.

I tried to finalize a barter with the manager at the Benbow Inn for a night's stay before I lost reception on Shelter Cove Road. Once I pulled up at the Whitethorn Construction yard and parked behind the winery, I saw Tasha wearing jeans, a grey t-shirt and a purple bandana. She greeted me tentatively before I went in for a hug. The memories of driving out here to work flooded my mind with happy waves of endearment. The thing with Tasha was that when there was work to do, there was an air of intensity. She was apparently running behind and needed the extra help.

"Taste all the wines and make sure they're okay to pour," she said, which is probably the nicest assignment any winery employee could ever be asked to carry out. I opened four different Pinot Noirs with the most antique wine opener I'd ever seen. The focus of the day would be the Alder Springs Vineyard in northern Mendocino County. She had corked up a bottle each of the Cabernet Sauvignon, Merlot, and Cabernet Franc from that Laytonville site before she blended the three together for her commercial release, just to see how the independent components held up on their own. All three had heavy black sediment on the underside of the corks, and the wines poured inky and thick, weighing down the glass as I swirled and assessed.

"So, how're these tasting?" she asked about the concentrated, handbottled creations.

"They are black, rugged, mountain wines," I said with a blackened smile.

Her face lit up. "I have to taste these then." She asked me what winery tasks I'd learned at Hirsch and Rogue River. I rambled off the night-and-day differences of production protocol and fermentation techniques; where Hirsch relied on all-natural yeasts and acids, Rogue River took no chances.

"You must be getting good then," she said with a smile.

"Oh, I don't know. Not really. I've learned a bunch."

We agreed that the Merlot was the heaviest, with noticeable alcohol (Tasha said it was in the 15.5% range) but rich and gushing with dark flavors and textures. The Cabernet Franc was my favorite, with a crazy herbaceous character and a chocolate mint nose, and the Cabernet Sauvignon was a stealthy tannic beast with years, if not decades, ahead of it.

Heather showed up at the winery right when Tasha's assistant Joseph and his wife Yani were chatting with me. I came around the tasting table and gave her a warm hug. It was amazing that she had made it all the way out here on her own. I introduced her to Yani, Joseph, and Tasha and poured her the first Chardonnay of the lineup, then every wine after that. She looked hotter than ever, wearing a tight black sweater and brown boots that slinked over her jeans to her knees. We didn't get out of there until close to six, with Heather getting a little tipsy and me buying close to two cases of wine.

* * *

What a high roller's tour of Humboldt County Heather and I had. From a night at The Benbow Inn (in which my wine barter for half a night's stay resulted in getting the Rogue River Syrah on their wine list), to dinner at Folie Douce in Arcata, and concluding with a lavish salmon feast on Sunday night when we had

Mourad's house all to ourselves. We did the emerald triangle in luscious, mostly naked style. We drank a bunch of good wines—2004 Peter Michael Chardonnay, 2001 Littorai Hirsch Pinot (thanks to David), Williams Selyem 1998 Hirsch Pinot against a Whitethorn Hirsch from the same vintage (both tired, with the Williams Selyem having a heavy buttery note and more new oak), and Heather's bright, delicious 2001 Clarendon Hills Blewitt Springs Grenache which we had at Folie Douce alongside a great pizza with apricot jam, mozzarella, brie, and salami. She bought that expensive wine at a shop in Carmel after hearing about my potential job in South Australia. I sprinkled money all over that county like I never had before and felt like a first-time tourist. It was fascinating to go back to a place where you lived when you were broke with a little disposable income. I felt like an entirely different character around these parts than I was when I was married, and it felt wonderful.

CHAPTER 39

With my harvest employment in the Rogue Valley slimming down and my tasks becoming less critical, I pointed out to Rob how we hadn't surfed together in Oregon yet. So Thursday night, after getting high and drinking a suspicious Italian Pinot Grigio that came in a shampoo container, I got online and checked out the weather, wind and swell forecast for Brookings, Oregon. A storm front was moving in Saturday, blowing out the coast through Tuesday, when 40-foot seas and 40-mile per hour south winds were filling in. It looked like if we were going to get an Oregonian surf in, it was going to have to be on Friday, and that would entail bailing on work.

Rob rubbed his hands together with a big, mischievous smile about the idea, while Katie held Dylan and sent her husband the silent, maternal look of urgency. Her concern was professionalism on Rob's part. He had just received a massive bonus check from Big Country and an offer of a brand new truck. Katie thought it'd look bad if we just blew off work to go surfing.

Rob realized this dream though. After a morning round of pump-overs, we hauled back to the house and got ready for our daytrip to Brookings. For Rob to prepare himself for our surf mission, he threw on gray sweatpants, athletic socks, and double-strapped sandals, then grabbed a sack of oranges, three foil-wrapped frozen burritos that he was going to cook on my hot engine while we surfed, a huge glass bubbler, bottles of water, and my bag of weed.

Our first view of the coast north of the Smith Rivermouth confirmed what I'd anticipated—offshore winds, moderate swell, and sunny skies. I floored it to Harris Beach. Some swell activity was crashing around the cinematic outer headland, but not as much as on Thanksgiving Day when the surf was maxed out. We dropped down into the state park loop and we saw the magic. The waves on the south cove were perfect in the golden afternoon sun. Finally, I'd nailed this spot. I surprised Rob with more enthusiasm than he'd seen from me in four weeks of working in his cellar.

"Oh my God," Rob said, seeing the complicated bay full of waves breaking sideways into normal waves, making them monstrous. I parked in a spot next to an older woman reading a paperback in a pickup truck.

"We need a more chronic-friendly parking spot," I said, reversing and parking further ahead. We got out and saw three to four different peaks breaking with nobody out or even looking at it.

"That is insane," Rob said, having never seen waves breaking like this. At first we considered paddling out at the south cove, with full side waves washing off the rockpile, but then a three wave set broke in the center of the bay, with lefts coming together in a perfect V shape and barreling and wedging through to the creek mouth.

I popped the hood for Rob to set the burritos on the engine, then we suited up and got in the truck for a hotbox in our wetsuits. The wind was unfortunately picking up, but it was blowing out of the north, so all of the lefts were breaking into offshore winds. Once on the sand, we noticed the surf was bigger than it seemed from the lookout. In fact, the south bowl was spitting and exploding, and as we made our entry, the south moving current started sucking us toward that rockpile.

"Let's do the left," I said. "But let's walk it." So we got out and walked up the beach to the creek mouth.

When Rob put his fins back on he said, "Yep, I look just like a big fat seal. I'm gonna get eaten."

"No you're not, man. You're fine here."

Our second attempt made for an easy paddle out. The straight view of the north cove painted the picture of a perfect left-hand pointbreak. Rob wasn't picking up on where the channel was, so he soldiered through each icy and powerful crashing wave, getting thrashed the whole way out and exhausted as a result of it. Meanwhile, in the channel, I didn't even have to get my hair wet. I was out there. After a harvest full of cellar work, I had the elasticity of Tony Bennett and my first wave put it well to the test. Paddling back out with an awestruck, open mouth, I passed by a set that reeled over that sandbar. This was as good as this beach gets, and we were here for it.

I tried to urge Rob into a few waves, but he kept telling me to go. I rode a long one across the bay, trying to glide into sections, my back sore but getting by. But then I paddled into a right-hand screamer and went full throttle into a ramp. I launched a 360-degree air off the back. Rob claimed I was seven feet up. "Man," he described it to me, "I was like 'D's flying through the air right now.'" Rob caught one wave finally, but he kept trying to paddle back out through the impact zone and got denied accordingly. However, he did have a perfect vantage point to see each of my 20 waves or so. I got a handful of dredgy in-and-out barrels and some snaps on the tentative side. It was frigid out in the water and the cold air didn't help.

My last wave wedged together on the sandbar, and after a late drop, I backdoored a barrel and got shot out. I avoided my customary cold water wetsuit flush and hobbled over to Rob at the tideline, the new pain in my back making itself known. He had been roaming ankle deep for awhile.

"You don't have to get out," he said.

"Yeah, but it's freezing though. And after that last one, I think I'm pretty done."

* * *

I awoke with a completely wrecked back the next morning. All that driving and surfing in cold water—and the cellar work itself—caught up with me. I wobbled around the Ashland Food Cooperative and spent $140 before I headed back to Rob and Katie's. I thought it'd be appropriate if I cooked something for them in lieu of the cheap $50 a week they'd been collecting from me. I picked up some Alaskan Cod and decided to do some Rogue Creamery raw cheddar and herbed mashed potatoes as the bedding. I bought a Chehalem Inox Chardonnay for $18 to go with it. Rob was still at work when I got back, but Katie and Dylan were home so I struggled in with my groceries and started chopping up ingredients for organic guacamole.

Rob got back and recounted the awkward social horrors of the wine club pickup party that I passed on.

I weighed myself after dinner and found I was up to 197, which was one pound under what I began harvest at Hirsch at. Crazy to think I was down to 185 during the peak of punch-downs on the Sonoma Coast. That's some good eatin' up in Oregon.

CHAPTER 40

"I just want the chunky nut peanut butt!" Rob sang to his daughter in front of their Christmas tree. Rob was sprawled out in his Eberle Winery long-sleeve shirt and plaid shorts, laid out by over 90 straight days of harvest work, his online gambling losses from the afternoon's football games, two bottles of wine, and a beefy dinner. He was nodding at the white-lighted Christmas tree, covered in sparkling ball ornaments and a red, jeweled strand spiraling around it, which the cats were nervous about. It was only six p.m. and I was feeling awfully self-conscious about drinking so much wine and for thinking it was a lot later than it really was on a Sunday. So I brewed up a concentrated French press to bring me back around. I'd already read both the *San Francisco Chronicle* Sunday edition and the slim *Oregonian* Sunday as I listened to the NFL onslaught that Rob had money on, devouring one snack after another.

"Okay, try this," I said, pouring Rob a taste of coffee, but again he refused. "Man, I just have to smell that shit and I have a turtle head poking out of my ass." I've never met someone who looked down on coffee so much. He equated his freedom from that addiction to Darwinian philosophy; as if when the world collapsed and it was every man for himself, he would go on to conquer the slumbering majority in caffeine withdrawal. I hadn't felt so self-conscious about drinking coffee. He believed coffee drinkers were the laziest employees and violators of company time. I was sneaking it at work, drinking it swiftly and out of sight. The best scrutiny-free spot was in the warm room trailer while stirring his Syrah barrels every morning, but only if you could keep the fruit flies out.

Later that night, I had a minor panic attack. It came on strong in the bathroom as I brushed my teeth and started pissing at the same time. My heart started pounding as I passed gas; it was like it was a poisonous gas and the lights went dim and my chest stiffened up and the sound muted. I made a break for the bedroom, opened the window and took in the fresh freezing air, crawling beneath the sheets. I called Mary, who didn't pick up, an unsympathetic Alex, and a liquored and concerned Heather. Was it the weed? Or was it a dietary flicker from that earthy Italian black truffle cheese I bought from the co-op? I was stuffed with beef, linguica, and Cold Stone Creamery, so it was hard to narrow down the source of this feeling.

And all I could hear in my head beneath those sheets was Rob's crazy mantra to his daughter: "Picklehead's got a big ol' head! Picklehead's got a big ol' head!"

* * *

I confessed my panic attack to Rob the next morning on the drive to the winery. I was making a joke of it, but I think it got to him. In light of its occurrence and the way I'd been eating, I got a Protonix prescription filled that afternoon—the first one since my birthday. I'd only taken 30 pills from June 19th through December 4th under the most strenuous and stressful of circumstances. I'd overcome my condition for the time being, without the daily use of any pills. It astounded me. I felt like an entirely new person every time I sat down to eat lunch or dinner. But here I was again, pushing the limits.

The tall older lady working the Gold Hill Pharmacy counter was concerned about how expensive the prescription was, even with insurance.

"It's better than not being able to eat anything good," I assured her.

Rob told Katie about my panic attack when we got home from work, and she was surprisingly empathetic, as if she'd been dying to have someone to relate to on the matter. "Darren, I know what you mean. I go crazy."

Still trying to downplay it, I said, "I think a lot of it was, you know, smoking all day, staying in, all the rich food." The last thing I wanted to do was blame their house and all the edible offerings. They'd been beyond accommodating. But Katie wanted to know details, so I brought it back to Rob's gas, all that food, then putting my toothbrush in my mouth, letting loose my own suffocating gas, then feeling my hearing go, my heart slowing down, and the broken record sound of "Picklehead's got a big ol' head!" being sung over and over.

We were laughing about it now. Rob offered more insight into it. "And you're juggling all that pussy! That ain't easy. What is it now, three chicks D? I remember. All those decisions. And you're like, 'Do I go to Australia? Do I work for Rob? Do I work for old man Hirsch? I got old pussy calling and new pussy calling.'"

Katie was with us on the conversation until Rob went off on the old and new pussy tangent. He was in sweatpants making a rich pot of clam chowder for our Chardonnay and Chowder night. He spent three hours cooking, even though Katie didn't like chowder. I opened up the Hirsch Chardonnay, which Rob really dug.

"That's nice wood, man. That's what I like." We drank his Rogue River alongside it, which was different stylistically, with less oak and more apple and tropical notes to it.

As I sat on the couch for my second bowl of chowder, Katie was on the computer and Rob kept advising me to "add Tabasco," "add salt," "add paprika." She turned around and started lampooning him in all of his OCD greatness.

"Darren, chew it longer. Darren, swallow more."

CHAPTER 41

It was my last week of Oregonian wine work. We'd pressed all the heavy red wines into tanks, then into barrels, and now the days were getting shorter. I spent the morning stirring barrels of Syrah in that heated container next to the winery, as well as the white wines in the back barrel room. The vineyard crew had been laid off. The wine harvest on all of the West Coast was coming to an end.

Rob came into the container and surprised me. "So, I've got the green light to bring you on." He and Guy had been in the office together talking since we'd gotten there that morning.

"Really? He's into me?"

"Let's talk about it, D."

"Well, they say the best business deals are made either on the golf course or in a strip club, and I can't golf."

Rob smiled big and rubbed his hands together.

We loosely comprised a plan to go to the gentlemen's club in downtown Medford called The Office that had a banner advertising a lunch buffet. Rob had heard good things, but had some hesitations.

"I'm scared to go in there, dude," he admitted.

"You're scared? Like, of running into a wine club member?"

"Nah," he squinted. "Of the methed-out ho's."

"Oh yeah, they probably are, huh?"

"Yeah, man."

"But who knows though," I said. "The Rhino in Santa Maria wasn't as bad as everyone said."

* * *

The instant we entered the house, Rob was greeted with a stressed out Katie on her cell phone and a diaper-loaded Dylan.

"Will you change her?" she said to him.

Without skipping a beat, he shrieked "Poopoo number twoskies?" and picked her up and changed her to give Katie a break.

"What are you gonna make for dinner, Mama?" Rob asked Katie when he was done. Dylan crawled out to the television, stood up, and pressed both palms to the big screen. The black cat named Hamlet looked around the room in an awkward stoniness. Rob didn't trust that cat.

"No, that black bastard is weird, man," Rob said about him. Rob hated all the stray cats that his wife fed outside, which had grown into a creepy army. One afternoon I saw Rob chasing down a sandal that had flown off after he went and kicked at one of them. "I'm gonna have to antifreeze them. Antifreeze Hamlet, antifreeze Roman. Kill 'em all."

Rob went into his bedroom to change, and I asked Katie if she'd ever been to the library in town. I'd given up on Henry Miller and was looking for a new book, and I assumed that the flashy new library a couple blocks down the hill had Wi-Fi access too. She sat on the couch shaking her head and from the bedroom we heard Rob start laughing.

"Did you really ask if Katie had gone to the library?" he asked.

"Rob, stop," she warned him.

"Darren, if there were ten big screen TV's on the wall, she might go in!"

"Rob."

"I'm not the library type either," he said. "I don't go to the library."

I walked down to the Gold Hill public library, which was in a nice, new corner building. There were outdated magazines on a rack, three empty computers, and two people in there. It was horribly overstaffed for the shift—three employees. As I tapped into the wireless connection, it hit me that I only had two days left in the state. I was going to miss hanging out with Rob's family and stuffing myself into oblivion every night. The five weeks had flown by, and as far as I knew, I'd been the perfect houseguest. My secret was never once having a bowel movement in Rob's house. It was a strange theory for my preservation at their place, but with only one toilet and Rob's affinity for spending a lot of time on there after work and at dawn, I thought of it more as a king's throne and kept it to the restroom at work. Not once did I slip on this and apparently it worked.

* * *

In an effort to eat healthier, I offered to cook a vegan dinner for the family. My five day tofu marinade approached perfection with the help of some color in the form of carrots and broccoli. I stir-fried the veggies, then blended them in with the local tofu, plopping that onto a bed of garlicky couscous with green onions and salt. We drank some Rogue River Viognier along the way.

"I feel the best this morning, dude," Rob said the next morning. It was a nice change to the beefed up, wine-soaked gut rot we'd been experiencing for five weeks now.

Patrick Comiskey from *Wine and Spirits* called and interviewed Rob about the noticeably rising quality of Southern Oregon reds, mainly the Syrah. So I asked him for Comiskey's direct email and fired off an inspired *Wine and Spirits* resume with references and three story ideas. I didn't mention Rogue River or Rob or being in South Oregon, though one of my story titles was "Rich South Oregon Reds." Coincidence or complete con? I got an email back asking for writing samples. I put a package together and got it out that afternoon.

As we sanitized the press before putting it to bed for the year, Rob started talking to me about my future. His motivational rant got my wheels spinning.

"Time to plant your feet in the ground, D," he said, rocking back and forth on his heels with his hands in his jean pockets, which I'd learned was his excitable, pre-sea turtle dismissal behavior. "I don't know, you might get by traveling from here to there, working at this cool place and that cool place. You might just get by. Me though, especially now with Dylan, I've gotta think about health care. I've gotta think about 401K. You might find yourself at thirty-seven all of a sudden with no savings and my belly and no bitches wanting to talk to you unless you've got that Bentley." He broke down how Big Country was putting 3% of Rob's salary into his 401K and how he would probably sell him bulk wine at half the price for his own label someday, just to keep him happy. He predicted how I'd probably start at 35K a year if I chose to work with him at Rogue River Vineyards, with a big bonus and health care and a 401K. After the surf fest at Harris Beach, I wasn't beyond living in Southern Oregon. I'd rent a room in Ashland or Medford, maybe buy a small home in Brookings to have as a surf shack. The idea was growing on me.

But what about the Hirsch scene? The great music, the killer wines, proximity to the ocean, traveling to flashy cities, meeting the chefs and wine directors, and eating at the finest restaurants now that my stomach had seemingly healed.

That was what I pictured after that talk with David. I was curious about what the prestige of being with a very famous vineyard was really worth.

I found myself boasting unintentionally to Rob after work about David's unbelievable record collection while answering a casual question in a weed-scrambled way about how I'd be spending my days at Hirsch when I returned on Monday.

"If you wanna listen to forty-fives, bro," Rob countered, "we can listen to forty-fives and drink as much 'Hermitage' as you can pronounce up here." Rob had cracked three of the Rogue River reds and I opened an Entrefaux Tardy Crozes-Hermitage that I had shipped up from William Cross Wine Merchants. The Frenchy didn't stand a chance after the fruit-driven and soft Rogue River trio. It came off as lean and dry until we tasted it later on, when it broadened out, seeming a little lusher.

* * *

The final day at Rogue River Vineyards arrived, and Rob and I were going to The Office to discuss business. Around ten a.m., as Rob went from tank to tank getting samples for the lab, he said, "Damn D, I'm ready to see some titty. Any titty!" He squinted, laughed, and rubbed his hands together eagerly. I was more intrigued by fulfilling a strange, lifelong curiosity of mine to actually see a real buffet in a strip club, with old pervs loading up plates of frozen mashed potatoes and deep fried everything between lap dances.

We finished up work and drove out of Gold Hill, taking the beautiful, wooded back way to Central Point along the Rogue River. It was a nice rural riverside route, with spacious houses that I didn't expect to see out there. Maybe it was the time of year, but Gold Hill didn't seem like much of a destination or a place where people would own vacation homes, but I guess they did. Rob explained all the nicer lawns and how people pumped river water up into their irrigation. It started becoming more and more of a privileged, albeit scandalous, job interview. Getting high made me nervous about going to a strip club. I had the same jittery anxiety rush that I got the first time I hooked up with a girl as a teenager, or even the time Willie wanted me to paddle out at Point Arena but it was just a little too big and I was ultra-caffeinated. I realized I'd never been to a strip club "dry," as Kris Kristofferson would say. On only coffee, a frozen burrito, and chronic, I was sort of freaking out.

Approaching downtown Medford, I pointed up ahead and said, "I see them twinklin' lights!" There was a parking spot right in front of the place and Rob took it. "Man," I said, "Jermaine Dupri wouldn't park his truck out in front of the club."

"I don't care, dude," Rob said, pulling his keys out of the ignition. "The only thing I'm mad about is that I'm not wearin' my sweats! Fuck!" He pounded the steering wheel. "How'd I forget?!"

We stepped out, just as the traffic light there turned red and trucks and cars piled up around us idling. People were checking out the two dudes going into the strip club in the daylight. We walked up to the corner entrance, just in time to cross paths with a woman pushing an infant in a stroller. She looked at me as I paused with a guilty hand on the door, then Rob broke that moral dilemma with "Go in, D. Go in." So I opened the door. We entered a small lobby with a register on a glass countertop and nobody working it. A sign read "Pay cover charge to bartender." A beady curtain partitioned us from the action. I looked at Rob questionably and he said, "You ready to do this?"

"Let's do it."

The beads clicked and swished as we entered the club. There was a main stage with a glossy pole, a DJ at the back left corner, six or seven pathetic men like ourselves on the $1 stools right in front, and some guys at the bar in conversation. I needed drinks—not *a* drink—to calm down, and it'd have to be something stronger than a beer. We sat up at the bar and the older, punk chick bartender took Rob's drink order of "Captain and Coke," and I dittoed it. The woman called me "sweetie" and "honey" amid the transaction as I got a twenty cashed into $1's. I looked like trash. I had my holey harvest work jeans on, my Clash T–shirt, wet socks and close-to-condemned Doc Martens that were ready to be tossed into a New Year's Eve bonfire.

As we got our drinks, a blonde girl with a back tattoo decked in a black leather skirt and matching bra, which loosely hung against her sagging, small chest, took the stage. I sucked on my drink. Rob thought his was weak. On stage, the girl practically gave her soul to every single one of those guys up there, rubbing herself into every greasy face, smoky mustache, and crusty mouth. I was repulsed on a sanitary level and still jittery as hell. I guess I had this illusion that strippers only really pounded it right into your face if you were either paying more than a buck a song for it or were handsome. I found myself *not* wanting her legs wrapped around my face, her post pregnancy belly grooving inches from my eyeballs.

Rob and I ended up talking business for about a half hour. Rob said he wanted me to earn my title—not just be moved up to assistant winemaker after putting in five weeks of work. He'd prefer I take the title "Cellar Master" first.

"Mainly 'cause *I* had to go to school and work my way up, goddamnit!" he said amid the thumping bass.

"Hey guys," one of the dancers said, coming right up to us and putting her hands on Rob's shoulders. She had the classic sweet aroma of stripper perfume. "What's up?"

"How's it going?" I asked her.

"Good. You guys looking for a dance?"

"Um, not quite yet 'cause we just got here," I said.

She kind of stood there. She was probably in her mid to late 20's and actually had good curves and sexy legs. I guess we were supposed to buy her a drink, but Rob wasn't having it. So after an awkward moment or two of strip club small talk, she said she'd see us later, and leaned in and gave me a hug. Over in a separate room to the left of the DJ was the private room, where I could see a couple old dudes getting grinded on. We quietly observed the depressing entertainment.

"So do I need to buy you a dance, D?" Rob asked, his glass drained as well.

"Man, I'm not really feelin' it," I confessed.

"Really? I was gonna get one, but now I don't know."

"Yeah, probably not a good call. I'm actually ready to leave whenever you are."

We'd seen the rotation of girls already and they were starting all over again on the stage. I wasn't having any of it, let alone the lunch buffet.

* * *

I can honestly say that I cried as I left Rob's house the next morning. I picked up a ceremonious double espresso from the drive thru coffee stand in Rogue River on my way west. I'd gained some weight, going as big as we did every night on the bottles and the cuisine, and I'd learned how to work smarter in the wine cellar. Rob had pounded into me how to run SO2's, acids, and alcohol levels in the lab, and I kept files on each task saved on my computer. I was moving along on the path to becoming a real winemaker. I didn't commit to taking the Oregon position just yet, as the Sonoma Coast and Australia awaited me. Rob told me to take my time in thinking it over.

CHAPTER 42

I felt warmly welcomed by the Russian River Valley with its houses and wineries decorated for the holidays. Guerneville had the look of downtown South Lake Tahoe, but without the snow. I pulled off at the Russian Rivermouth lookout in Jenner and saw a flat ocean. On my way up Meyers Grade, I experienced a combination of hominess and apprehensive stress about the next day's task of labeling the "M" Pinot Noir, now that David, Marie, and Mick agreed on the name and the label. What was supposed to be a couple weeks of housesitting was becoming work. We'd already bottled the wine in August and sent it to a cold storage facility in Santa Rosa. Our crew was going to go to the warehouse in the morning, set up our labeling machine, unpack some 400 cases of wine, then label them, repack them, and wrap each pallet.

Déjà vu hit around twilight when I crossed the cattle guard onto David's property and passed Yulí and Rígo's trailer. I'd always known this property while it buzzed with people, tractors, forklifts, chaos and hard work; now the air was cold, the vines nearly naked, and the winery deserted.

I charged down past blocks seven and nine toward the house. The gate was closed. I cracked it open, drove through it, and closed it behind me, driving down to the lower loop where David's truck and Marie's BMW were parked as usual. I opened the front door of the cottage, which looked exactly like I'd left it. There was a bottle of wine with a note on the counter. It was a bottle of Failla Syrah from Barbara, which I'd told her during harvest that I wanted to try, and had made an attempt to buy a bottle through Mike since he was trucking grapes to the winemaker Ehren Jordan. The handwritten card that came with the gift made me cry. She had truly looked out for me, especially during those horrible, awkward moments with Mick, and I really had connected with her family.

I unloaded my truck and started stocking my refrigerator, then opened my laptop and pressed play on The Band. David knocked a short while later and I greeted him while the song "Mystery Train" came on. He thanked me for arranging to come back in time to label the "M," and was all smiles. He invited me to dinner, then mentioned how the place felt cold. He adjusted the heater to get it going then turned to leave, but he paused and threw a thumb out toward the laptop. He smirked at me knowingly.

"It's the theme song for the ranch," I said.

"Who is that?"

"The Band. Off *Moondog Matinee*."

"Oh, well, that was an off-the-wall record. Huh. I need to check that out again. Okay, I'll see you at seven or a little before."

I made the bed and cleaned the bathroom until it was time to walk down. I cracked a Whitethorn Demuth Vineyard Pinot Noir and brought it over with Levon Helm's *Dirt Farmer* CD that I'd raved to David about in an email.

"Yeah, come in!" he announced from the couch. He had a thick black trench coat on over his usual getup. I came in and saw Marie was in the kitchen, and I awkwardly kissed her on only one of the two cheeks she presented French-style. There was a nice fire going in the wood stove. I showed them the bottle of Whitethorn. Marie handed me a glass of Chardonnay, and I took it over and sat in a chair across from David. He was as mellow as I'd ever seen him, petting Bobés on his lap.

"So, how'd it go up there in Oregon?" David asked. "Where were you again?"

"Southern Oregon. The Rogue Valley."

"Oh yeah. You know, I got some vines from a guy out in Cave Junction. Some one-fourteen vines. He brought the cuttings back from Burgundy himself."

"It was a lot different though. Making wine at this place. We had Pinot, but also Syrah, Cabernet, Merlot. We had one day where we processed seventy tons of Merlot and I just had to stand there at the crusher distributing scoops of sulphur and French oak powder."

"You hear that Marie? We should be doing that with the Bohan Dillon!"

"The stuff smells so good."

"Hey, let's put on that uh, Levon Helm CD. What do you think Marie? A little what do they call it, rhythm and blues?"

"Sure," she said, surrendering her Ukrainian electronica beats. She served the pasta carbonara and we sat and ate to *Dirt Farmer*. Marie gulped down her glass of Whitethorn and David did the same. He reiterated how Tasha was the only person he'd sell fruit to outside of his existing clients. He then talked about corporate grapefarming, his routine of leaving early to get a paper when he's in Czech, and recent independent films of interest. Close to nine he started to tune out. He drew me a map to the labeling fiasco at Alexander Valley Cellars. As we stood by the door upon my forthcoming exit, Marie mentioned how David's niece saw a female spirit in the cottage when she tried to sleep in it during Thanksgiving.

"She is a very sensitive girl," Marie clarified, "but we totally believe her. She ran out of the place one night and totally chose to sleep on the floor in our house instead of in there."

"Well, if it's a female spirit, then you'll have to excuse me now," I joked. "Where was she during harvest when I needed her most?" I said goodnight and headed out.

* * *

I pulled up at the gigantic, climate-controlled building and saw Mick's truck, Barbara's truck, and the vineyard crew all hanging out by one of the big roll ups. Mick smiled and shook my hand, and I hugged Barbara and shook hands with all the guys. I thanked Barbara for the Failla.

We got the "M" Pinot labeled and sealed up in about seven hours. I gave Barbara my two camouflage and buck printed Rogue River Vineyards hats for her and Mike, as well as a bottle of Rogue River Pinot Gris. She wasn't going out of town for Christmas after all, but was happy to have two weeks off of work at the winery.

I helped Mick load the labeler up into the back of his truck, then gave him the pound of organic dark roast I got for him at Muddy's in Humboldt. He asked me what my plans were. I didn't really have any, aside from getting back to the vineyard.

"You wanna have a beer?" he asked.

"Sure. Where at?"

"Follow me. We'll drop this labeler off at Davis Bynum and then go to Ace's."

Traveling behind him, I called up Trevor to tell him I was back and to see if he wanted to meet up at Ace's with us.

* * *

After a few pints with Mick, it was off to the Underwood for some small plates and a bottle of Radio-Coteau with Trevor. He decided to stay up on the ridge for a night with the promise of being delivered back to his truck the next day. I hadn't called Mary to tell her I was back, but we'd emailed. She said she had two of her girlfriends staying with her all week. Once on Seaview Road, I turned down the reggae and asked Trevor how he'd like crashing a house party of three girls.

"I've got a bottle of Mendocino Riesling that'll blow their minds!" he shouted over the beats.

"I should just send you up to the door first," I plotted. "No, Mary would probably call the cops."

"Fuck you!"

I smartly drove past the turnoff to the Seaview vacation rental and continued down to Fort Ross school. We took the secret road in style, and my driving had Trevor buckling back up. Getting back to Hirsch around 10:30, Trevor laid out the sleeping bag on the hard floor while I lounged back in bed. We smoked, drank the rest of the Crozes-Hermitage that I had open, and watched *Last King of Scotland* until it skipped out. He complained about the floor and tried to crawl up onto the edge of the bed.

"Not happenin' man," I told him.

* * *

At around 7:15 a.m., I heard David say my name from the front porch.

"Hey Darren, we gotta be on the road by eight."

"I'll be there in fifteen minutes," I said. He was going to show me where the generator was in case it stormed as hard as it did the previous year when the ranch lost power for days on end.

"I left you some wine here," he said.

I was still medicated by all the previous night's provisions as I pushed myself up and used the bathroom. When I came out, I saw that Trevor had brought in Bobés the cat and two grocery bags full of wine.

"You're stoked, bro," he said, laying out on the white bookshelf in chronological order a four year vertical of Wild Hog Pinot Noir, and three wines from Pine Ridge in Napa Valley.

I did the walk around with David, wished him a nice trip, and returned to the cottage to get ready to head into town. After rushing Trevor back to his truck, I picked up some groceries at Andy's Market, then retreated back to the ranch and fell back asleep.

I woke up to silent sunshine a little after noon.

I brewed coffee and took a shower. Contemplating my apparel for the day, I first chose jeans like I had somewhere to be, then retreated to flannel pajama pants. I filled a thermos with coffee, grabbed a mug and a guitar, and hit the back deck. I played music for a couple hours, started writing a song, then quit to have some lunch. I got a tofu marinade going, then splashed the rock cod I bought with the juice, cut up some fingerling potatoes, and brought everything and the Failla Phoenix Ranch Syrah down to the Hirsch's. Around three, I was eating frozen mozzarella mushroom bites and polishing off the rest of the Pine Ridge Rutherford Cab, before pouring the Failla into a massive Riedel Grand Cru Burgundy glass that I found in the cabinet. I simply sat and huffed on that Syrah in such extravagant, hand blown stemware. An hour later, I rinsed it out with hot water, then delicately went to polish it with a paper towel and the stem broke clear off and slashed my finger open. I was scared, holding this huge stemless goblet in one hand and the bloodied stem in the other. David was not going to be pleased. I added getting a replacement to my Christmas shopping list.

Afterwards, I got a good wood fire going. At one point the fire was going so good that I saw a huge cloud of smoke blocking out the landscape through the window. I went outside and saw thick smoke plowing out of the chimney. Was the house on fire? David would kill me if his place burned down. His cellar and record collection consumed by fire? I'd be dead and bastardized in *Wine Spectator* as the stoner that burned down the most famous Pinot Noir vineyard in the state. With that paranoia in mind, I ashed the fire down a bit.

I called Heather later that night, and we formulated a quick weekend trip up here. This corner of the ranch would be rock n' rolling soon enough.

* * *

On a rainy Saturday afternoon in the Hirsch winery barrel room, Heather took her shirt and bra off while I was topping the barrels. Maybe it was when we got into the block six lots—with the delicious French forest faceoff of Allier versus Troncais—that she felt the urge to go bare-chested. I juggled the wine thief, stemware, and two very pink, stiffened nipples. Dr. John sang "gonna get a little frisky" on his *Gumbo* album, and that's just what we did every morning and night she was here. What an ass I was becoming. The girl was gorgeous and smart, with zero baggage, and she earnestly liked me, yet I found myself slowly deciding that I needed to end it and leave it as what it was—a sparkly, lavish, hedonistic and financially irresponsible waltz down a neon, abbreviated lane. We all need spotless memories, or more so, memories of spotless times. There aren't many. There's always a smudge or a fingerprint.

With Nate and Trevor showing up unexpectedly on Sunday, I had to give Heather a lot of credit for hanging in there for a rainy, eight-hour Big Brother and the Holding Company backstage style hangout. My brick of hash was being vacuumed by Nate. Meanwhile, Heather graciously opened bottles of Kistler and Kosta-Browne, which Trevor bashed for no reason, and I offered the vertical of Wild Hog that turned out to be horribly flawed and rancid in its entirety. The hash ball was diminished in girth, and they smoked close to an eighth of my Humboldt.

On Monday morning, after dropping Heather off at her car, I came back and the guys were being tame—Nate was even doing dishes. We had breakfast before they asked me about my plans for the day. Trevor wanted to surf, and he selfishly wanted us to all take my truck. The roads were muddy, so we'd be resigned to Bohan Dillon Road, and I didn't want to burn up my gas.

"I'm cool with drinking wine here all day," Nate admitted, standing tableside while Trevor and I read the paper and drank espresso. "Is that cool with you, Darren?"

"If you guys want to stay, you've gotta contribute something. The old rosé isn't cutting it Nate, and," I paused to point at Trevor, "he's gonna eat all of my food."

Trevor sighed and looked back down at the paper to avoid the spotlight. "I'm down to get a bottle at the store," Nate said. "I don't have much cash so it'd have to be cheap."

"Can't wait to try that," I said. Trevor laughed and Nate started to smile. They left an hour later without me.

* * *

I was listening to Bob Dylan's *Planet Waves* on vinyl, drinking a bottle of Whitethorn Hirsch Pinot and reading *Wine Spectator* when Minka the cat jumped up onto the chair behind my back and started attacking me. Perturbed, I turned out the lights in the house and headed back up to the cottage. At around 10:20 my phone rang, which out at Hirsch doesn't even qualify as a booty call. Those sorts of lusty calls begin at six p.m. and end at eight out here, usually under the traditional premise of "What're you doin' for supper?"

It was Mary. The fatherly side of me answered with, "Are you okay?"

"Yeah. Do you want to come by the winery tomorrow?" she asked.

"Really?"

"It's Neil's last day before he goes to Europe, so he said it'd be cool if you came by and tasted the wines."

"Really? He said that?"

"Yeah." A long pause followed. "How come you didn't tell me you were back?"

"I don't know."

"That's not cool, man."

"I got back this weekend," I lied.

"Whatever. I have your jacket and the rosé to give you."

"Oh, okay."

"They're tasting at eleven. He said you could sit in on that too."

* * *

It rained three inches overnight, and I paid close attention to the wind in hopes that the storm wouldn't hit extreme status. I slept comfortably in spite of the weather, thanks to the 15.5% alcohol Whitethorn bomb. I got up at 8:30 and ran through the rain to let Bobés and Minka out and to feed them. I started to boil water for coffee when my phone rang with "Seaview Winery" on the caller ID. I picked up. Mary was in the close company of Neil and Ethan, so she spoke in professional mode. She let me know that if I was to come to the tasting, that I had to be there by 10:30. That didn't leave me much time. It was only two miles away, but it took 25 minutes when the roads were good.

I threw on some clothes and took a muddy Bohan Dillon Road to Seaview. Outside of the winery, there was a long-haired guy in a tie-dye shirt clearing holes in the drain by the parking spots. I went into the offices and saw no one at the desks, so I started down the hallway.

"Hey guys," I announced as I walked in to the lab.

Neil was wearing a beanie and a vest, and we shook hands. "Man, we made you drive over in the worst weather," he said, giving me a big smile. I greeted Ethan, who was seated at his computer entering in the sort of paperwork that Mick handwrote through the harvest. Mary declined hand or hug and kept on with her "cork soaking experiment," which entailed sinking new corks from different manufacturers in little shot glasses filled with a ten percent vodka solution. Neil was sniffing each glass after a soak for evidence of the dreaded cork taint, often abbreviated by TCA (Trichloroanisole). The corks with the least amount of taint would be the ones Seaview would order for an upcoming bottling.

The General Manager John came in later as I was checking my email on Mary's computer, so I got up and shook hands with him. Ethan printed out tasting sheets, and then Mary set up the Reserve Pinot Noir tasting in the next room.

"So we're going to taste first, then we'll come in and get you," she said. "It can be really intense sometimes."

I took advantage of a civilized internet connection and YouTube'd the video of Bob Dylan and Mark Knopfler playing "License to Kill" in a studio in 1982. Soon I was invited in, and I tasted through a Pinot Noir flight. Their categories were rated on appearance, aroma, taste, finish, and food to pair with. One wine had that stemmy Russian River Valley note, with buttery herb and chronic overtones. Then I tried two other reserve wines. I told Neil about David's flawed vertical of Wild Hog Pinot, then how I'd emailed David and asked him if I could get into a couple bottles of the "M" and got denied. Neil laughed and said, "We'll give ya some wine, Darren."

After the tasting and a snack in the break room with the Seaview crew, Mary had me drive her over to the vacation home to get the two gallon containers filled with rosé that we made together. I tasted the wine in the vacation house's kitchen. It came out extracted looking and dark, like a red wine. Maybe letting the skins sit for three days was too much? The nose was good, but the palate was filled with a sour, acidic finish.

Her reception was chilly. Things had changed. When I dropped her back off at Seaview, she coldly said "Good luck with everything," then she shut the door and walked back into the winery.

I had two Carlo Rossi jugs full of fermenting, underripe rosé in my truck. It wasn't the first time I found myself at the end of harvest driving around with complete homemade shwag in my vehicle and a woman who was over me.

CHAPTER 43

On December 23rd, I packed up my belongings, fed the cats and refilled their water bowls, watered the houseplants, drove away from the Hirsch estate, and closed the gates behind me. I was on my way to Mick's house in Napa for dinner and a sleepover. I never hung out with him outside of work (with the exception of those pints at Ace's), and I imagined his haven was his home, with his wife Anne, Cornelius, their cats he'd talked about, and all of his music around.

I drove through downtown Calistoga before dark, following his directions into a residential neighborhood. I passed the fairgrounds and drove down a quaint, tree-lined street. I arrived at a modest two-bedroom house with a tiny yard. After knocking on the door, Anne greeted me with a hug and said that it was good to see me. She was making bacon wrapped figs in my honor, and immediately poured me a flute of Roederer Estate. A vegetarian glazing their fingers with raw bacon for a carnivorous dinner guest is like a greasy mechanic whipping up some cashew seitan for a surprise vegan at his barbecue. She'd heard of my claim that bacon twice a day was what accounted for me being the only worker who didn't get sick during harvest. I set down a bottle of Whitethorn Demuth Vineyard on the counter top.

"Mick is out getting mushrooms from the grocery store," she said. "He'll be back in a bit." There were some hand drums in the corner of the living room and no television set. She talked about the different cats that were roaming about, and the upcoming Orange County trip with her parents.

Mick got there and we shook hands and got reacquainted. He poured himself a glass of sparkling wine and the talk turned to music. Mick went fishing for an album we were chatting about. More wine flowed.

We sat at the dinner table, listened to Gillian Welch, and had a spicy salad with a Pride Viognier that surprisingly didn't have me rushing to the restroom with acid overload. My condition from a mere five months ago didn't even cross my mind. We had mushroom pasta with a kelpy, oyster brine flavored Whetstone Hirsch Pinot, and my Whitethorn, which surprisingly was on the volatile side and smelled of nail polish remover.

They both thanked me for sticking it out at Hirsch, with Anne joking that she can't even live with Mick during harvest.

"Hey now," he said, "come on."

"It's true!" she teased him.

They asked if I was considering coming back. I shared David's offer and some of my concerns before ultimately getting into my failed marriage story with Anne, who guessed my ex was undergoing changes in life that I wasn't. "You guys were really young for marriage. Not that it's easy at any age," she added.

Anne retired to bed after the Port and cheese course, which my stomach handled pill-free and with ease. Mick put on a CD by The Be Good Tanyas and refilled our glasses. He toasted me for doing as many punch-downs as I did and provided a grave warning about being safe in confined spaces if I was going to work in Australia. He wasn't keen on the idea of spending so much of my own money to go down there and work, and he questioned if the Aussies that employed these foreign cellar hands were taking advantage of the system by not pitching in for the work visa. Maybe they were. He elaborated on the danger of confined space again, and the massive, closed-top tanks that were so commonly used in Australia for Shiraz fermentation.

"Be careful," he said with a long look. It was true: cellar workers died in tanks from carbon dioxide nearly every year in some wine region of the world. The more and more I thought about it, the more I was ready to disappear in France and spend my money on surfing the beaches of Hossegor. I was more likely to do just that instead of going broke to bust my ass all over again for a winery on the other side of the planet.

He got up and started washing some dishes. I asked him if he needed any help and he declined. We'd drunk a small river, and I looked haggard at best, standing in the kitchen all red-eyed as he scrubbed away bacon and fig residue from a pan. He put two fingers to his eyes and then pointed at the French press on the counter.

"In the morning, help yourself. We're a press house, so, you know." It brought up the memory of him calling Turley Vineyards a "wild house," referring to a winery that uses wild yeasts like us. It reminded me of the old school restaurateur lingo of my father, where everything was a something house. In fact, Mick reminded me more of my father than I'd realized, which explained a lot of things.

"Thanks so much for dinner, Mick. And for everything. I learned a lot. As crazy as it was. But thanks."

"You're welcome," he smiled and did a spastic nod. We shook hands there in his kitchen in the Napa Valley. Then his tone changed, his face grew serious, and we released the handshake. "Sleep well," he instructed me, just like it was that first night in the trailer when we had a 16-hour workday ahead of us.

* * *

I drank a strong, grainy cup of coffee on the morning of Christmas Eve and hugged Mick goodbye. It was cold outside, nearly frozen in Calistoga, and my head was swollen with sulfites. The sun was shining somewhere. I rattled out of the residential onto an icy Highway 29, discovering that the Napa Valley was practically deserted. The leaves on the grapevines were crinkled and the color of fire, if hanging on at all anymore. The slick, black trunks of an ancient Zinfandel vineyard resembled a ragged army of howler monkeys. I was the only vehicle on a highway so often congested with wine lovers of the world searching for that thrilling bottle or, mostly, the next link in the chain of inebriation. I sped up some, put my sunglasses on, turned on The Band's *Music From Big Pink*, and drove toward the next adventure.

ACKNOWLEDGEMENTS

I would like to express my sincere gratitude to the real-life characters in this book who have colored and enriched what was a turbulent stage of my existence. I am sincerely blessed to have had your company. My heart goes out to the Hirsch family for giving me this rare opportunity to live on their vineyard, work harder than I thought I could, and mend and mature myself on their sacred mountain. Thanks to the Furlong family for treating me like their own and, most importantly, the meat and the onions. I am seriously humbled by my editors Abby Blank and Andy Maness who machete-slashed through my humiliating first draft in return for some excellent wine, which, in the end, is what it's all about.